RETAIL SELLING SKILLS

Sumit Kati

First Edition : 2010

Himalaya Publishing House

MUMBAI • NEW DELHI • NAGPUR • BANGALORE • HYDERABAD • CHENNAI • PUNE • LUCKNOW • AHMEDABAD • ERNAKULAM • BHUBANESWAR • INDORE

First Edition : 2010

Published by : Mrs. Meena Pandey
for **HIMALAYA PUBLISHING HOUSE PVT. LTD.,**
"Ramdoot", Dr. Bhalerao Marg, Girgaon, **Mumbai - 400 004.**
Phones: 2386 01 70/2386 38 63, Fax: 022-2387 71 78
Email: himpub@vsnl.com
Website: www.himpub.com

Branch Offices:

New Delhi : "Pooja Apartments", 4-B, Murari Lal Street, Ansari Road, Darya Ganj, **New Delhi - 110 002.** Phone: 23270392, 23278631
Fax: 011-23256286

Nagpur : Kundanlal Chandak Industrial Estate, Ghat Road, **Nagpur - 440 018.**
Phone: 2738731, 3296733 Telefax : 0712-2721215

Bangalore : No. 16/1 (Old 12/1), 1st Floor, Next to Hotel Highlands, Madhava Nagar, Race Course Road, **Bangalore - 560 001.**
Phone : 22281541, 22385461, Telefax: 080-22286611

Hyderabad : No. 3-4-184, Lingampally, Besides Raghavendra Swamy Matham, Kachiguda, **Hyderabad - 500 027.** Phone: 040-65501745
Mobile : 09848130433

Chennai : No. 85/50, Bazullah Road, T. Nagar, **Chennai - 600 017.**
Phone: 044-28144004/28144005

Pune : First Floor, "Laksha" Apartment, No. 527, Mehunpura, Shaniwarpeth, (Near Prabhat Theatre), **Pune - 411 030.**
Phone: 020-24496323/24496333

Lucknow : C-43, Sector - C, Ali Gunj, **Lucknow - 226 024.** Phone: 0522-2339329

Ahmedabad : 114, "SHAIL", 1st Floor, Opp. Madhu Sudan House, C.G.Road, Navrang Pura, **Ahmedabad – 380 009.**
Phone: 079-26560126, Mobiles: 09327324149,09314679413

Ernakulam : 39/104 A, Lakshmi Apartment, Karikkamuri Cross Rd., Ernakulam, **Cochin – 622011**, Kerala.
Phone: 0484-2378012, 2378016, Mob.: 09344199799

Bhubaneswar : 5 Station Square, **Bhubaneswar (Orissa) - 751 001.**
Mobile: 9861046007, E-mail:- orissa@himpub.com

Indore : Kesardeep Avenue Extension, 73, Narayan Bagh.Flat No. 302, IIIrd Floor, Near Humpty Dumpty School, Narayan Bagh, **Indore (M.P.)**
Mobile: 09301386468

DTP by : HPH, Editorial Office, Bhandup (Priya)

Printed by : Heram Graphics, Bhandup

PREFACE

Today all across the world we are seeing a growth in the disposable income. People across societies and cultures are becoming brand conscious as well as accepting retail malls/superstores/multibrand stores as a part of their everyday lives.

People are also diverting towards these big stores because they are finding these big stores more attractive and full of varieties. Second, many big retail stores are entering every market of India (big or small).

The main advantage which people find with these chains is that they get the entire requirements from single place, therefore, now people can easily buy all important things of their requirements from the single place.

This entire situation could become even more competitive with the time and entry of big players Wal-Mart, etc. Retail boom in India is now going stay for long time and we can even that future also belong to big stores.

We have all heard about the famous principle 'Customer is King', to add on to this in today's scenario "Every customer is a King". There is nothing called as a big customer and small customer every customer is important. One should also keep in mind, gone are those days when the products and services used to be sold merely by themselves. With the competitive world one should keep in mind everything good or bad needs to be sold, today without selling nothing sells. Thus, putting more pressure on the people behind the sales counter's and the people on the store floor. In short retail associates need to establish a rapport with a customer quickly. Offering to provide assistance and asking pertinent questions are effective openers and can usually help the associate gauge the customer's interest. But maintaining the customer's interest, and developing a relationship takes a little more work.

Selling is a skill with and appropriate blend of indispensable knowledge, I have incorporated the perfect mix of both along with a pinch of the attitude which is required to succeed as a retail sales personnel.

This book will help an individual to become a better retail salesperson. There is a huge reflection of concerns and the possible solutions which a person could use in the daily scenarios. I have incorporated the solutions using the day-to-day real store floor realities, which is very evident in the examples used as well as the tips provided.

This book will act as a quick and crisp reference for the practical points for day-to-day usage for all individuals.

Sumit Kati

CONTENTS

1.	Introduction to Retailing	1 - 24
2.	Requirement Mapping for Retail Sales	25 - 46
3.	Customer Identification and Approach	47 - 62
4.	Customer Needs Identification	63 - 77
5.	Importance of Product	78 - 96
6.	'Buying' — A Memorable Experience	97 - 110
7.	Closing a Sale	111 - 124
	Case Study	125 - 158

Chapter 1
INTRODUCTION TO RETAILING

Objectives

After going through this chapter, you will be able to understand:

- The Scope of Retail Industry in India
- The employment opportunities in Retail Sector
- Various store formats
- Key concerns of Retailers

Structure:

1.1 What is Retailing?

1.2 Retail in India

1.3 Retail Sector in India – Employment Opportunities

1.4 Retail Formats

1.5 Key Challenges

1.6 Concerns of Retaliers

1.7 Summary

1.8 Self Assessment Questions

Retail means selling goods and services in small quantities directly selling to customers. Retailing consists of all activities involved in marketing of goods and services directly to consumers for their personnel family and household use.

1.1 "WHAT IS RETAILING?"

The word "Retail" originates from a French-Italian word. Retailer–someone who cuts off or sheds a small piece from something. Retailing is the set of activities that markets products or services to final consumers for their own personal or household use. It does this by organizing their availability on a relatively large-scale and supplying them to customers on a relatively small-scale. Retailer is a person or agent or agency or company or organization who is instrumental in reaching the goods or merchandise or services to the end-users or ultimate consumer.

The retail sector has played a phenomenal role throughout the world in increasing productivity of consumer goods and services. It is also the second largest industry in the US in terms of numbers of employees and establishments. There is no denying the fact that most of the developed economies are very much relying on their retail sector as a locomotive of growth. The India retail industry is the largest among all the industries, accounting for over 10 per cent of the country's GDP and around 8 per cent of the employment.

The retail industry in India has come forth as one of the most dynamic and fast paced industries with several players entering the market. The retail sector has played a phenomenal role throughout the world in increasing productivity of consumer goods and services. It is also the second largest industry in the US in terms of numbers of employees and establishments. There is no denying the fact that most of the developed economies are very much relying on their retail sector as a locomotive of growth. Retailing involves all activities incidental to selling to ultimate consumers for their personnel family and household use. It does this by organizing their availability on a relatively large-scale and supplying them to customers on a relatively small-scale. Retailer is any person/organization instrumental in reaching the goods or merchandise or services to the end-users. Retailer is a must and cannot be eliminated.

1.2 RETAIL IN INDIA

Retailing is the most active and attractive sector of last decade. While the retailing industry itself has been present since ages in our country, it is only the recent past that it has witnessed so much dynamism. The emergence of retailing in India has more to do with the increased purchasing power of buyers, especially post-liberalization, increase in product variety, and increase in economies of scale, with the aid of modern supply and distributions solution.

Indian retailing today is at an interesting crossroads. The retail sales are at the highest point in history and new technologies are improving retail productivity though there are many opportunities to start a new retail business, retailers are facing numerous challenges.

The Indian retailing industry is becoming intensely competitive, as more and more payers are targeting for the same set of customers. The major retail players are Pantaloon Retail, Shoppers' Stop, Reliance, etc. Retailing is one of the biggest sectors and it is witnessing revolution in India. The new entrant in retailing in India signifies the beginning of retail revolution. India's retail market is expected to grow tremendously in the next few years.

In India, the most of the retail sector is unorganized. In India, the retail business contributes around 11 per cent of GDP. Of this, the organized retail sector accounts only for about 3 per cent share, and the remaining share is contributed by the unorganized sector which is mostly a family-owned business in India.

The main challenge facing the organized sector is the competition from unorganized sector. Unorganized retailing has been there in India for centuries, these are named as mom-pop stores. More than 99% retailers function in less than 500 sq. feet of area.

All the merchandise was purchased as per the test and vim and fancies of the proprietor also the pricing was done on *ad hoc* basis or by seeing at the face of customer. Generally, the accounts of trading and home are not maintained separately. Profits were accumulated in slow moving and non-moving stocks which were to become redundant or consumed in-house. Thus, profits were vanished without their knowledge. The manufacturer were to distribute goods through C and F agents to distributors and wholesalers. Retailers happen to source the merchandise from wholesalers and reach to end-users. The merchandise price used to get inflated to a great extent till it reaches from manufacturer to end-user. Selling prices were largely not controlled by manufacturers. Branding was not an issue for majority of customers. More than 99% customers are price sensitive and not quality or brand sensitive at the sametime they are brand conscious also. Weekly bazaar in many small towns was held and almost all the commodities were on the scene including livestock. Bargaining was the unwritten law of market. Educational qualification level of these retailers was always low. Hence, market was controlled by handful of distributors and/or wholesalers. Virtually there was only one format of retailing and that was mass retail. Retailer to consumer ratio was very low, for all the categories without exception. Variety in terms of quality, styles were on regional basis, community based and truly very low range was available at any given single place. Almost all the purchases/(buying) by mass population was need-oriented and next turn may be on festivals, marriages, birthdays and some specific occasions.

Impulsive buying or consumption is restricted to food or vegetables, etc. Having extra pair of trousers or shirts or casuals and formals and leisurewear and sportswear and different pair of shoes for occasions is till date is a luxury for majority population except for those living in metros. Purchasing power of Indian urban consumer is very low and that of branded merchandise in categories like apparels, cosmetics, shoes, watches, beverages, food, jewellery, are slowly seeping into the lifeline of Indian city folks. However, electronic and electrical home appliances do hold appropriate image into the minds of consumers. Brand name does matter in these white goods categories. In the coming times also majority of organized retailers will find it difficult to keep balance with rest of the unbranded retail market which is very huge.

The India retail industry is the largest among all the industries, accounting for over 10 per cent of the country's GDP and around 8 per cent of the employment. The retail industry in India has come forth as one of the most dynamic and fast paced industries with several players entering the market. But all of them have not yet tasted success because of the heavy initial investments that are required to break-even with other companies and compete with them. The India retail industry is gradually inching its way towards becoming the next boom industry.

The total concept and idea of shopping has undergone an attention drawing change in terms of format and consumer buying behaviour, ushering in a revolution in shopping in India. Modern retailing has entered into the retail market in India as is observed in the form of bustling shopping centres, multi-storied malls and the huge complexes that offer shopping, entertainment and food all under one roof.

A large young working population with medium age of 24 years, nuclear families in urban areas, along with increasing working women population and emerging opportunities in the services sector are going to be the key factors in the growth of the organized retail sector in India. The growth pattern in organized retailing and in the consumption made by the Indian population will follow a rising graph helping the newer businessmen to enter the India retail industry.

In India the vast middle-class and its almost untapped retail industry are the key attractive forces for global retail giants wanting to enter into newer markets, which in turn will help the India retail industry to grow faster. Indian retail is expected to grow 25 per cent annually. Modern retail in India could be worth US$ 175-200 billion by 2016. The food retail industry in India dominates the shopping basket. The mobile phone retail industry in India is already a US$ 16.7 billion business, growing at over 20 per cent per year. The future of the India retail industry looks promising with the growing of the market, with the government policies becoming more favourable and the emerging technologies facilitating operations.

Source: Article written by Mr. Achal Arya Director of Acumen Education Group - Management Institute in Delhi

The main advantage in unorganized retailing is consumer familiarity that runs from generation to generation. It is a low cost structure; they are mostly operated by owners, has very low real estate and labour costs and has low taxes to pay.

In late 1990s the retail sector has witnessed a level of transformation. Retailing is being perceived as a beginner and as an attractive commercial business for organized business, i.e., the pure retailer is starting to emerge now. Organized retail business in India is very small but has tremendous scope.

Organized retailing will grow faster than unorganized sector and the growth speed will be responsible for its high market share, which is expected to be $ 17 billion by 2010-11.

Retailing will show good prospects in cities like Mumbai, Delhi, Chennai, Kolkata, Banglore and Kanpur. After Dubai, Singapore and Hong Kong, in India Delhi will be the next big retail destination. According to Confederation of Indian Industries whose findings have shown that Delhi has the good resources and good conditions for the retail sector. Out of the total earnings of the Government of Delhi Rs. 11,000 crore, Rs. 6,500 crore is achieved from the retail sector.

The organized sector is expected to grow faster than GDP growth in next few years driven by favourable demographic patterns, changing lifestyles, and strong income growth. This organized retail sector mix includes supermarkets, hypermarkets, discounted stores and speciality stores, departmental stores.

India with such a population will have its own consumption levels very high and with the increase in the disposable income the retailers are bound to do well. The growth of the retail sector will act as a fuel to the growing Indian economy. Some of the benefits to the economic growth are as mentioned below:-

- Better quality products and services would lead to better competition
- More exports bring more foreign direct investments
- Organized Indian retail sector would encourage tourism
- Along with the employment boom there would be a vast development in the expertise of the human resource

There would remain future scope for improvements in agriculture, small, and medium scaled with the help of the Indian retail sector

Some of the key growth drivers in India for retail sector are as follows:

(1) Rising incomes and improvements in infrastructure are enlarging consumer markets and accelerating the convergence of consumer tastes.

(2) Liberalization of the Indian economy

(3) Increase in spending per capita Income.

(4) Advent of dual income families also helps in the growth of retail sector.

(5) Shift in consumer demand to foreign brands.

(6) Consumer preference for shopping in new environs.

(7) The internet revolution is making the Indian consumer more accessible to the growing influences of domestic and foreign retail chains.

(8) Reach of satellite T.V. channels is helping in creating awareness about global products for local markets.

(9) The increasing share of young population in total population of India.

(10) Availability of quality real estate and mall management practices

(11) Foreign companies' attraction to India is the billion-plus population.

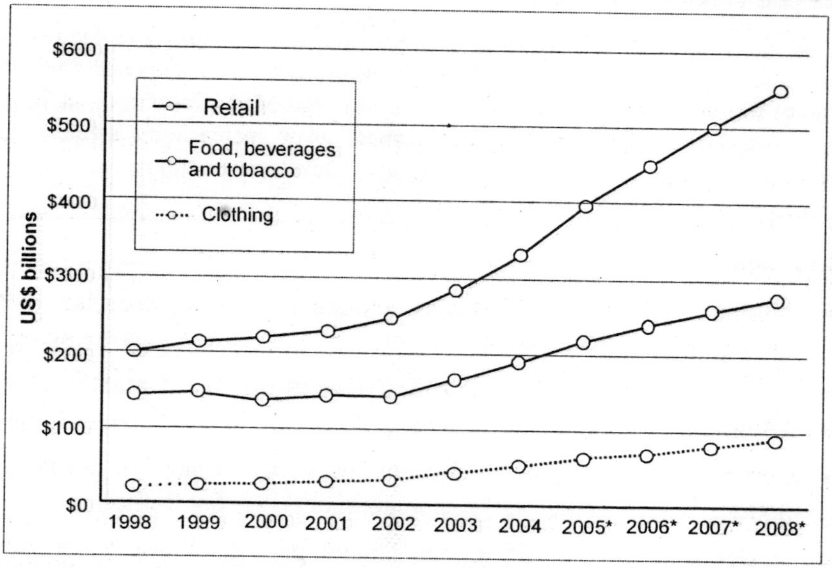

Source: Economist Intelligence Unit and A.T. Kearney analysis

*Data for 2005-2008 is based on estimates

INDIA IS THE MOST ALLURING MARKET FOR GLOBAL RETAILERS

By siliconindia news bureau

Wednesday, 17 June, 2009, 15:54 hrs

Bangalore: India has been ranked as the most attractive nation for retail investment by U.S.-based global management consulting firm A T Kearney. This survey was done between 30 emerging markets and India surpassed countries like China, Russia and the United Arab Emirates. India has become the most attractive destination for retail investment for the fourth time in five years.

India was followed by Russia on the second spot and China on third, while United Arab Emirates and Saudi Arabia were placed at fourth and fifth respectively. Few countries have improved from their previous rankings. India improved its position from number two spot last year to become the leader.

The report also says that "In India, slower retail sales are causing Indian retailers to delay expansion plans and restructure their operations. But this has opened a window of opportunity for global retailers and many firms like Wal-Mart, Carrefour and Tesco are continuing expansion plans as Indian consumers grow increasingly affluent, brand-conscience and familiar with global retail formats." Developing countries are expected to be the ones who will lead the economic recovery.

Some key points

- Retailing in India is witnessing a huge revamping exercise as can be seen in the graph
- India is rated the fifth most attractive emerging retail market: a potential goldmine.
- Estimated to be US$ 200 billion, of which organized retailing, (i.e., modern trade) makes up 3 per cent or US$ 6.4 billion
- As per a report by KPMG the annual growth of department stores is estimated at 24%
- Ranked second in a Global Retail Development Index of 30 developing countries drawn up by AT Kearney.
- Multiple drivers leading to a consumption boom:
    - Favourable demographics
    - Growth in income
    - Increasing population of women
    - Raising aspirations: Value-added goods sales
- Food and apparel retailing key drivers of growth
- Organized retailing in India has been largely in urban
- Phenomenon with affluent classes and growing number of double-income households.
- More successful in cities in the south and west of India. Reasons range from differences in consumer buying behaviour to cost of real estate and taxation laws.
- Rural markets emerging as a huge opportunity for retailers reflected in the share of the rural market across most categories of consumption.

* ITC is experimenting with retailing through its e-Choupal and Choupal Sagar in the rural hypermarkets.
* HLL is using its Project Shakti initiative for leveraging women self-help groups to explore the rural market.

1.3 RETAIL SECTOR IN INDIA — EMPLOYMENT OPPORTUNITIES

Any industry or a sector which booms provides a lot of employment opportunities, thus in turn acting as a fuel in the growth of the country's economy. Infact more employability gives more and more people increased disposable income which is basic growth requirement for exponential growth of the retail sector. Some reports say, after agriculture, retail is the largest source of employment and has deep penetration into rural India.

The increase in the number of consumers twinned with the introduction of organized sector has brought numerous corporate investments in retail sector. The entry of supermarkets, enormous departmental stores, and shopping malls has encouraged the retailers to look at new business plans of expansion.

An economic growth on a monumental scale is offered by the Indian retail sector, equally in the national and international market which in turn will generate a huge source of employment and a variety of options for the consumers. The Ernst & Young's report 'The Great Indian Retail Story', anticipates that the Indian retail sector would come up with 2 million employment opportunities within the year 2010.

The present employment in the retail business is nearly 4 crore and around 20 crore depends on this sector. There is a scope of better exposure to the international standards with the entry of transnational companies, which in turn is encouraging more and more retail management programmes to open up and help bridging the gap of supply and demand of talented professionals for management.

Retail companies are starting retail management courses in partnership with management institutes, roping in talent from other sectors and developing comprehensive career growth and loyalty plans for existing employees.

Top players like Pantaloon Retail India Limited, Trent, Shoppers' Stop, RPG Group and Ebony are virtually on their toes.

Consider the plans of largest player, the Pantaloon Retail India Ltd., the company has developed a comprehensive strategy, wherein it expects that in 2 years, it will not recruit any new managers from outside.

Pantaloon on a cosmetic change

PRIYANKA SANGANI
Mumbai, 3 February

Having established itself as a major player in the retail space, Pantaloon Retail is now foraying into the services area with an entire range of diagnostic healthcare centres and beauty salons.

The first of the salons, Star and Sitara, will open in Bangalore in March and is aimed at the same profile of customers who visit a Big Bazaar outlet.

"Any customer who is comfortable in a Big Bazaar will feel at home here as well," says Kishore Biyani, managing director, Pantaloon Retail. "Health and beauty forms about 10 per cent of a consumers expenses, and we intend to capture part of that outgo," he added.

In addition to the salons, Pantaloon will also be setting up diagnostic centres offering eye, skin and dental treatments among others.

Rahul Bhalchandra, head - wellness, Pantaloon Retail, however, says they are not looking at a hospital kind of a set up, but more of preventive care. "We wont have emergency rooms but will be more oriented towards preventive and maintenance care," he explains. The centres will also include fitness centres, gyms, pharmacies, beauty retail centres as well as alternative treatments like ayurveda and homeopathy. Bhalchandra was previously head of Health and Glow, the RPG group venture.

"We will be setting up the wellness centres within the malls that Kshitij (a Pantaloon promoted company) will be constructing. In addition to the wellness centres, there will also be smaller standalone units like just pharmacies or cosmetic retail outlets within our other stores which we will start opening by March," says Bhalchandra.

Managing director Kishore Biyani says the company will target the same customer profile who visits Big Bazaar outlets, for beauty and wellness centres

"The estimated need is 1 lakh of employees till 2011", said Mr. Sanjoy Jog, HR Head of Pantaloon Retail India Ltd. Pantaloon has the concept of partnership with educational Institute to run retail courses across the entire chain. The company has tied-up with eleven-Bussiness schools including K J Somaiya, Welingkars, Narsee Monjee and IISWBM. "The students join the course and they are given an appointment letter by Pantaloon to become employees" said Mr. Jog, Pantaloon. Pantaloon is also planning to tie-up with Ahmedabad-based National Institute of Design to start a course in visual merchandising. "The apex body of Indian organized retailers, Retailers Association of India(RAI) is also lending help hand to tide over the shortage of employees in organized retail sector.

Trent has also started in-house learning programmes and now goes to under graduate colleges to recruit students.

Since, the job market is hugely receptive to this with more and more business schools focusing on the sector and large retailers setting up retail academics.

The retail sector not only opens employment opportunities for the management graduates, but a lot of opportunities come up for other less formally educated people as well. As it is common sense when a particular supermarket is opened one would not only require store managers but a lot of people would be required as helpers, delivery boys, back office people, feet on floor sales people. This also drives a parallel economy of suppliers, vendors, drivers, and many more. In short, the retail boom will have direct as well as indirect employment advantages.

> **THE TIMES OF INDIA**
>
> **Service sector rides high on retail boom**
>
> 8 Apr, 2007, 0048 hrs IST, THE NEW DELHI: India's booming economy, growing middle-class and increasing disposable income is fuelling a retail boom in the country. And, following close on the heels of this boom are cold-chain suppliers, software providers and educational institutes that are expected to benefit directly from it. The rapid growth of modern retailing, especially in food and groceries, calls for an organised cold-chain infrastructure. India is one of the largest producers of fruits and vegetables in the world. Moreover, India's food market is valued at $70 billion, which is doubling every three years. Air-conditioning and refrigeration major, Carrier, is already providing refrigeration equipment for long-distance trucks and trailers for delivery of perishable products. Similarly, Ingersoll Rand's solutions include pre-cooling, cold storage and land transport refrigeration. It's already supplying refrigerator systems to large retail chains in India. "We see a multi-fold increase in the refrigeration business in the coming years. Right now, less than 10% of the fresh produce goes through a cold-chain," says Daljit Mirchandani, president, Ingersoll Rand (I) Ltd. Retail players in education are hiring by the dozen and soon this number is expected to surpass the IT and BPO sectors. MeritTrac, a company specialising in assessments, recently released a survey on skill requisites of retail sales personnel. The study noted that an executive rated half as good as his colleague on creative presentation skills, loses out on 25% of all sales opportunities his colleague is certain to succeed in. The survey also said that sales personnel lack the key skill to explain creatively and demonstrate the product. India is currently facing a shortage of 3,00,000 skilled retail (both frontline and experienced) professionals. Keeping this in mind, NIIT Imperia has launched a set of programmes targeted at executives. The IT major, in association with IIM-Calcutta, is planning programmes in the arena of retail management. With organised retail requiring substantial investment in technology, IT providers and software players are developing solutions specific to the sector. Sun Microsystems' Java CAPS is an integrated platform that enables real-time application connectivity and data synchronisation. Globally, Sun's turnover from the retail sector is over $1 billion. "Most retailers in India are looking at inventory management solutions," says Priyadarshi Mohapatra, GM, retail practice, Sun Microsystems India.

1.4 RETAIL FORMATS

The format of a retailer is the overall appearance and feels that it presents to customers, primarily its look and layout, the sort of range its stocks and the approach taken to pricing.

Format is distinct from fascia which, strictly speaking, refers solely to external appearance. Retailers occasionally use it as as a synonym for format.

The format, together with range, pricing and marketing, is one of the key determinants of a retailer's success. Of these, the format is very often the hardest to get right. A good format will both draw in customers and help present products well to generate sales.

Mom-and-pop Stores:

These are generally family-owned businesses catering to small sections of society. They are small, individually run and handled retail outlets.

Category Killers:

Small speciality stores have expanded to offer a range of categories. They have widened their vision in terms of the number of categories. They are called category killers as they specialize in their fields, such as electronics (Best Buy) and sporting goods (Sport Authority).

Malls:

The largest form of organized retailing today located mainly in metro cities, in proximity to urban outskirts. Ranges from 60,000 sq. ft. to 7,00,000 sq. ft. and above. They lend an ideal shopping experience with an amalgamation of product, service and entertainment, all under a common roof. Examples include Shoppers' Stop, Piramyd, and Pantaloon.

Speciality Stores:

Chains such as the Bangalore based Kids Kemp, the Mumbai books retailer Crossword, RPG's Music World and the Times Group's music chain Planet M, are focusing on specific market segments and have established themselves strongly in their sectors.

Discount Stores:

As the name suggests, discount stores or factory outlets, offer discounts on the MRP through selling in bulk reaching economies of scale or excess stock left over at the season. The product category can range from a variety of perishable/non-perishable goods.

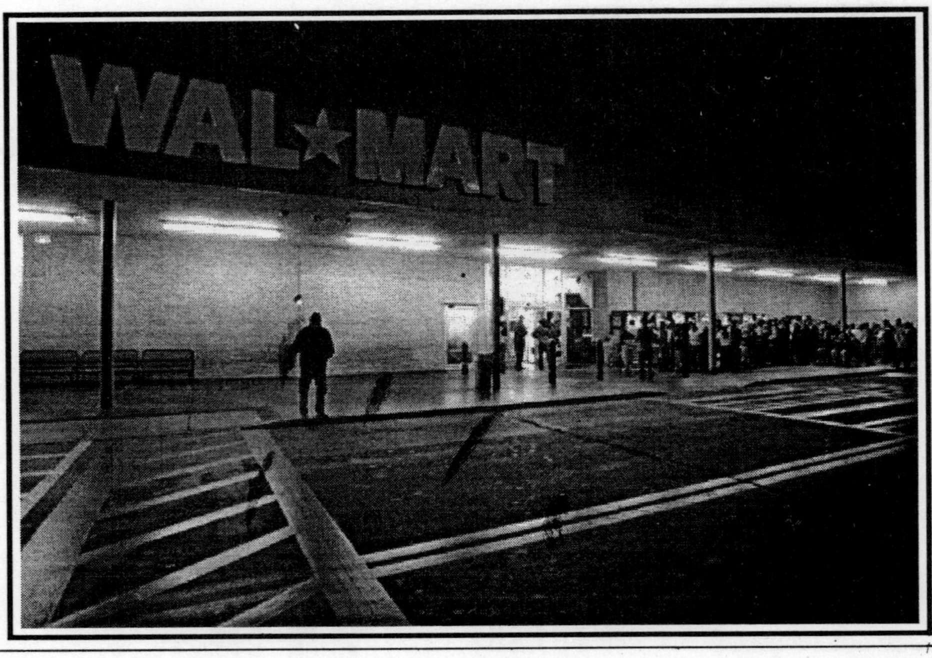

Departmental Stores:

Large stores ranging from 20,000-50,000 sq. ft. catering to a variety of consumer needs. Further classified into localized departments such as clothing, toys, home, groceries, etc.

Departmental stores are expected to takeover the apparel business from exclusive brand showrooms. Among these, the biggest success is K Raheja's Shoppers' Stop, which started in Mumbai and now has more than seven large stores. (over 30,000 sq. ft.) across India and even has its own in store brand for clothes called Stop.

Hypermarts/Supermarkets:

Large self-service outlets, catering to varied shoppers' needs are termed as Supermarkets. These are located in or near residential high streets. These stores today contribute to 30% of all food and grocery organized retail sales. Supermarkets can further be classified in to mini-supermarkets typically 1,000 sq. ft. to 2,000 sq. ft. and large supermarkets ranging from of 3,500 sq. ft. to 5,000 sq ft. having a strong focus on food and grocery and personal sales.

Convenience Stores:

These are relatively small stores 400-2,000 sq. feet located near residential areas. They stock a limited range of high-turnover convenience products and are usually open for extended periods during the day, seven days a week. Prices are slightly higher due to the convenience premium.

MBOs:

Multi-Brand outlets, also known as Category Killers, offer several brands across a single product category. These usually do well in busy market places and metros.

E-tailers:

These are retailers that provide online facility of buying and selling products and services via internet. They provide a picture and description of the product. A lot of such retailers are booming in the industry, as this method provides convenience and a wide variety for customer. But it does not provide a feel of the product and is sometimes not authentic. Examples are Amazon.com, Ebay.com, etc.

Vending:

This kind of retailing is making incursions into the industry. Smaller products such as beverages, snacks are some the items that can be bought through vending machines. At present, it is not very common in India.

Key Challenges for Retail in India

SLUMP-HIT RETAILERS LOOK TO SMALL TOWNS FOR RELIEF

Vishnu Pandey, Kanpur, March 02, 2009

Business Standard

Slowdown-hit retailers in Uttar Pradesh are now targeting customers in tier-II and tier-III towns to make up for the loss in footfalls in the overreached metropolitan cities. Retailers such as Future Axiom and Vmart have decided to consolidate their business by reaching out to unexplored markets outside major cities, believing them to have been relatively unaffected by the downturn.

Future Axiom's mobile bazaar CEO, Ashy Sehgal, said tier-II cities in India are reporting significant growth and it has become crucial for every retailer to build a strong presence in these cities.

"We have evolved a two-pronged strategy to capture the untapped market and smaller towns. One, we are working on a franchisee basis to enter these markets and, secondly, we are also working on standalone models based on our strengths and feasibility," he said.

Future Axiom will be opening another 1,000 stores by December 2009 and suite a few of these stores will be opened in the smaller cities. Quite a few tier-III cities seem to have the potential to provide recent returns. The growing middle-class in tier-II and tire-III cities have decent disposable income," Sehgal said.

"We believe that the employment opportunities in these cities will grow further resulting in better purchasing power and amplified opportunities for us. The telecom and hosiery retailers are not experiencing significant slowdown as of now," he added.

When asked about the prospects of ongoing recession slowing down returns, he said that the group was all set to expand and widen its reach with 1,000 new stores being planned. "Indian mobile retail industry is still very exciting and is not experiencing significant slowdown as of now," he explained.

He further said that residents in smaller towns were mostly earning their livelihood from government jobs or farming-based activities, which have not been hit by the slowdown as severely as the larger cities. Instead of spending heavily on attracting more customers in overreached metropolitan markets, we can target the unheeded customer waiting for us in smaller cities," he argued.

Agra-based construction firm Baba Constructions has recently built a shopping mall in Etawah, a town with a population of less than four lakh, and has similar offers to construct malls in smaller markets like Farrukhabad, Muzzafarnagar and Sitapur.

Vivek Agnihotri, joint director of the firm, told Business Standard that cost of its retail ventures were based on the franchisee model and even international brands such as Reebok opened their stores here.

Another retail giant Vishal Mega Mart has also opened its store in smaller cities like Etawah. Some 18 shopping malls are expected to be shifted from big city centres to smaller towns or the low-cost suburban areas adjoining the main cities.

1.5 KEY CHALLENGES

(1) Location:

"Right Place, Right Choice"

Location is the most important ingredient for any business that relies on customers, and is typically the prime consideration in a customers store choice. Locations decisions are harder to change because retailers have to either make sustainable investments to buy and develop real estate or commit to long-term lease with developers. When formulating decision about where to locate, the retailer must refer to the strategic plan:

- Investigate alternative trading areas.
- Determine the type of desirable store location
- Evaluate alternative specific store sites

(2) Merchandise:

The primary goal of the cost retailers is to sell the right kind of merchandise and nothing is more central to the strategic thrust of the retailing firm. Merchandising consists of activities involved in acquiring particular goods and services and making them available at a place, time and quantity that enable the retailer to reach its goals. Merchandising is perhaps, the most important function for any retail organization, as it decides what finally goes on shelf of the store.

(3) Pricing:

Pricing is a crucial strategic variable due to its direct relationship with a firm's goal and its interaction with other retailing elements. The importance of pricing decisions is growing because today's customers are looking for good value when they buy merchandise and services. Price is the easiest and quickest variable to change.

(4) Target Audience:

"Consumer the prime mover"

"Consumer Pull", however, seems to be the most important driving factor behind the sustenance of the industry. The purchasing power of the customers has increased to a great extent, with the influencing the retail industry to a great extent, a variety of other factors also seem to fuel the retailing boom.

(5) Scale of Operations:

Scale of operations includes all the supply-chain activities, which are carried out in the business. It is one of the challenges that the Indian retailers are facing. The cost of business operations is very high in India.

1.6 CONCERNS OF RETAILERS

Retailers are faced with many issues as they attempt to be successful. The key issues include:

- **Customer Satisfaction** – Retailers know that satisfied customers are loyal customers. Consequently, retailers must develop strategies intended to build relationships that result in customers returning to make more purchases.
- **Ability to Acquire the Right Products** – A customer will only be satisfied if they can purchase the right products to satisfy their needs. Since a large percentage of retailers do not manufacture their own products, they must seek suppliers who will supply products demanded by customers. Thus, an important objective for retailers is to identify the product customers will demand and negotiate with suppliers to obtain these products.
- **Product Presentation** – Once obtained product must be presented or merchandised to customers in a way that generates interest. Retail merchandising often requires hiring creative people who understand and can relate to the market.
- **Traffic Building** – Like any marketer, retailer must use promotional methods to build customer interest. For retailers a key measure of interest is the number of people visiting a retail location or website. Building "traffic" is accomplished with a variety of promotional

techniques such as advertising, including local newspapers or internet, and specialized promotional activities, such as coupons.

- **Layout** – For store-based retailers a store's physical layout is an important component in creating a retail experience that will attract customers. The physical layout is more than just deciding in what part of the store to locate products. For many retailers designing the right shopping atmosphere, (e.g., object, light, sound) can add to the appeal of a store. Layout is also important in the online world where site navigation and usability may be deciding factors in whether of a retail website is successful.
- **Keeping Pace with Technology** – Technology has invaded all areas of retailing including customer knowledge, (e.g., customer relationship management software), product movement, (e.g., use of RFID tags for tracking), point-of-purchase, (e.g., scanners, kiosks, self-serve check-out), web technologies, (e.g., online shopping carts, purchase recommendations) and many more.

THE GREAT INDIAN RETAIL MELTDOWN: A KPMG STUDY

Saturday, June 13, 2009 08:00 IST

Our Bureau, Mumbai

After an upward growth for the last five years, India's retail sector has started to lose steam. In a survey by consultancy form KPMG, 70% of the respondents stated that the slowdown has adversely affected footfalls. Apart from this, poor conversion ratios have led to declining sales growth figures - 11% in December 2008 compared to 35% in December 2007.

The study, Indian Retail: Time to Change Lanes, looks at the changing contours of the retail industry and examines the drivers that are likely to have an impact across various categories of the sector. It focuses on how these drivers are affecting various players across the retail value-chain and suggests strategies that could help them cope with the situation.

The survey expects the current slowdown to last 12-18 months conditional on government incentives in increasing expenditure on infrastructure, development initiatives and other activities to stimulate the economy. "We believe that players who take immediate strategic measures will be the dark horses. Be it store rationalisation, change of supply-chain management, consolidation of operations or improvement in IT infrastructure - retailers need to think quickly to protect their margins and become tougher for more challenging times," says Neil Austin, KPMG's global head of marketing.

It is expected that there will be an increased focus on value retail in the coming months and a shift away from lifestyle goods. Food retailing and FMCG products are likely to continue to grow since commodities here remain largely insulated from the slowdown.

Closing unprofitable stores, the rationalization of capital expenditure and opting for low rent premises will be short-term focus areas for retailers.

The KPMG survey also revealed that while attracting customers was one of the top concerns for retailers, investment in consumer research was not amongst one of their top priorities. The market watchdog believes that companies that invest in customer relationship management and consumer research analysis would stand to gain against those who take customers for granted.

Way forward:

If numbers are to be believed, India's retail industry is estimated at about USD 350 billion and forecast to be double by 2015. As per Associated Chambers of Commerce and Industry of India (ASSOCHAM), the overall retail market is expected to grow by 36%. Growing consumerism would be a key driver for organized retail in India. Several demographic trends are favourable for the growth of organized trade.

- ***Rapid income growth:*** Consumers have greater ability to spend.
- ***Increasing urbanization:*** Larger urban population which values convenience coupled with higher propensity of the urban consumer to spend
- ***Growing young population:*** Growth of post liberalization maturing population with the willingness to spend (attitude)
- ***Tendency to spend now:*** Consumers willing to borrow for current consumption

As per one of the reports from Tata Strategic Management Group (TSMG) in the next 10 years, the overall retail market in India is likely to grow at a CAGR of 5.5% (at constant prices) to 1,677,000 Cr in 2015. The organized retail market is expected to grow much faster at a CAGR of 21.8% (at constant prices) to Rs. 2,46,000 Cr by 2015 thereby constituting ~15% of the overall retail sales. Based on our projections, the top 5 organized retail categories by 2015 would be food, grocery and general merchandise, apparel, durables, food service and home improvement.

Retailers inspired by the Wal-Mart story of growth in small town, America are tempted to focus on smaller towns and villages in India. However, a careful analysis of the town strata-wise population, population growth, migration trends and consumer spend analysis reveals a very different picture for India.

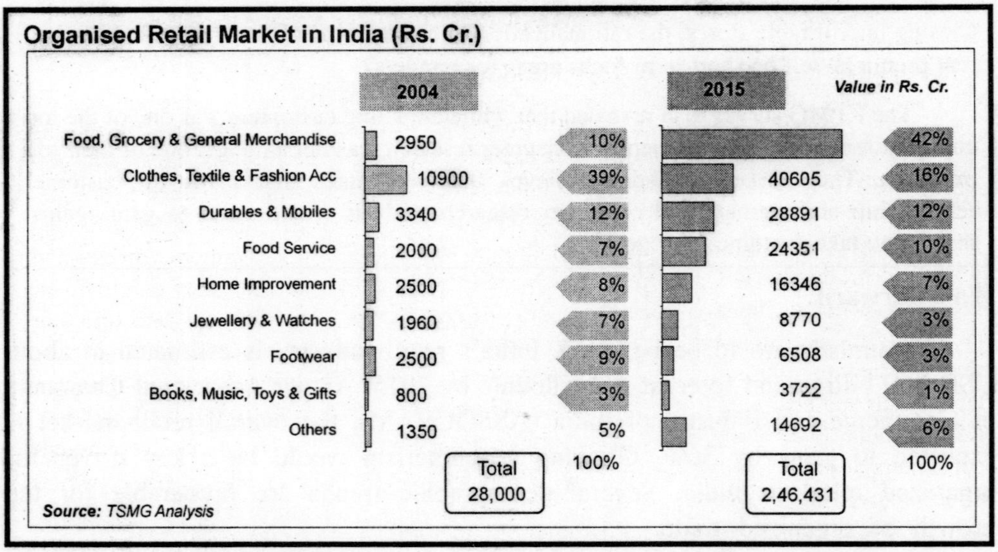

As per the estimates, the share of the 35 towns with current population greater than 1 mn in the overall population of India would grow much faster from 10.2% today to reach 14.4% by 2025. Simultaneously, the share of these towns in the overall retail market would grow from 21% today to 40% by 2025.

Within these top 35 towns, an estimated 70-80% of trade could be in the organized sector. This is similar to the experience in China where in cities like Shanghai and Beijing, organized sector accounts for 70-80% of overall retail trade in certain categories.

Hence, retailers should focus on the top 37 towns in the next decade. The opportunity in smaller towns and rural India would be smaller and fragmented as compared to the larger town.

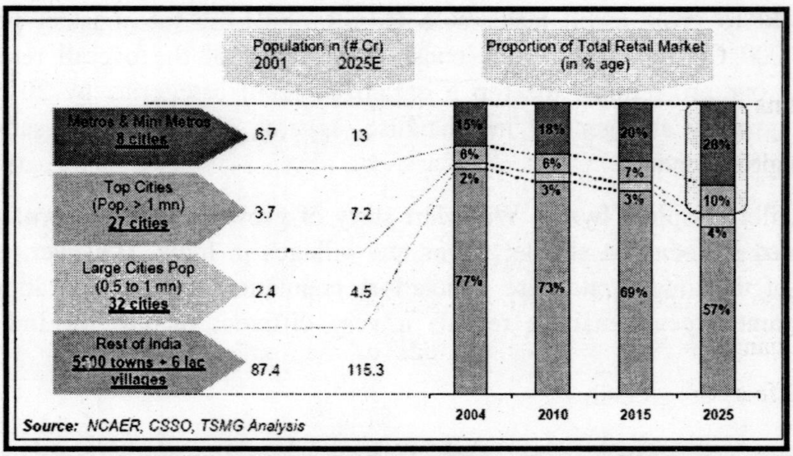

RURAL INDIA PROMISES GROWTH FOR RETAIL

8 April, 2009, 0126 hrs IST, Rupali Mukherjee, TNN

NEW DELHI: There may be a slowdown in urban retail, but 'Bharat' is still shining for retailers. The next phase of growth is expected to come from rural markets with rural India accounting for almost half of the domestic retail market, which is valued over $300 billion. Rural India is set to witness an economic boom, with per capita income having grown by 50% over the last 10 years, mainly on account of rising commodity prices and improved productivity. Development of basic infrastructure, generation of employment guarantee schemes, better information services and access to funding are also bringing prosperity to rural households. "Overall there is a huge market which is waiting to be served, ready to splurge, willing to explore new products and services, and retailers can tap on their wallets," said Ramesh Srinivas, national industry director (consumer markets), KPMG India. In rural markets, consumers are practical and price sensitive. Even though consumers at the bottom of the pyramid do not seem to have predictable income (which affects purchasing dynamics), the rural market proved to be surprisingly loyal. So if companies get it right they could really reap the rewards, experts added. This is particularly true as changes in the rural economy such as people moving from agriculture into manufacturing, which pays better, are likely to lead to a economic boom. In order to earn brand loyalty in the rural market, product design will need to go beyond ideas like smaller sizes (such as single use sachets) to create genuinely new products that appeal to this segment. "This requires a deep understanding of the market and an appetite for innovation, posing a challenge for both consumer products companies and retailers as there is still lack of shared understanding about the ever-changing Indian market and types of consumers that make it", says Pinakiranjan Mishra, leader retail and consumer products, E&Y India. Also, with most of the retail markets in cities getting saturated, rural markets offer a sea of opportunity for retailers. Retailers have devised different models to serve rural markets. For instance, ITC promoted 'Choupal Sagar' has a hub-and-spoke model involving farmers. "The model offers a rural shopping mall where they can sell their commodities and can buy almost anything including garments, cosmetics, electronics and even tractors," says a KPMG report. Other examples include Pantaloon Godrej's joint venture (Aadhar), Reliance Retail (Fresh and Fresh Plus), Hindustan UniLever (Shakti), DCM (Hariyali Kisaan Bazaar) and Mahindra & Mahindra (Shublabh).

Key reasons for growth of retail companies in India:

1. Existing Indian middle-classes with an increased purchasing power
2. Growing economy
3. Large young population
4. Rise of upcoming business sectors
5. Change in the taste and attitude of the Indians
6. Effect of globalization

7. Heavy influx of FDI in the retail sectors in India
8. Increase in number of International Brands available in Indian market.

1.7 SUMMARY

India with a large young population and a promising GDP growth is mainly depending on the self-consumption concept. And with all the things in the right place retail in India will be a big time expansion. This will not only provide employment to urban Indian, but create lakh of job at the front end. With retail booming, it will give opportunities in the secondary peripheral industry like logistics and many more. Although with all the challenges and hurdles India will be the next big destination for all the global retailers.

1.8 SELF ASSESSMENT QUESTIONS

1. Explain in short various retail formats present in your city.
2. Explain in short the unorganised retail in India.
3. With the help of a retailer in your vicinity finds out the various job opportunities available in retail.
4. Explain in retail the major concerns for a retailer in India.

2

Chapter

REQUIREMENT MAPPING FOR RETAIL SALES

Objectives

After going through this chapter, you will be able to understand:

- Importance of SWOT for self
- How do a SWOT for self and use the same
- The important traits required to the successful in retail sales.

Structure:

2.1 Introduction

2.2 SWOT

2.2.1 Theory for SWOT

2.2.2 Personal SWOT analysis

2.3 Few Important Traits for a Success in Retail Sales

2.3.1 Creating a positive first impression

2.3.2 Communication skill

2.3.3 Empathy

2.3.4 Objection handling

2.3.5 Knowledge

2.3.6 Being assertive

2.3.7 Managing anger

2.4 Summary

2.5 Self Assessment Questions

2.1 INTRODUCTION

Every person on this globe is a salesperson, at some on the other time in life everyone sells.

As a child haven't we tried to sell an idea to our parents, of why they should buy us a chocolate or a new toy or send us for on picnic or buy us a new dress or shoes? Similarly, on the day of school or college admission we had to package and sell ourselves to the concerned authorities. Some people call it persuasion, but at the end what one is trying to do is sell. Thus, the fact is that every person needs to be seller — and a seller to be successful.

Every profession requires some skill sets similarly there are some vital qualities and skill sets to be successful salesperson. In our context to retail selling also there are some traits, which a person requires to have. In this chapter we will discuss sell analysis, thus to help us know ourselves better and mop our traits to the essential traits required for a successful salesperson in a retail perspective.

2.2 SWOT

Every person should be and aware of his/her strengths and weakness. This will not only helps in self-analysis but will also give a fair idea about the potential threats and opportunities. Let us first understand the SWOT (strength, weakness, opportunity and threat) analysis.

SWOT analysis is a powerful technique for identifying Strengths and Weaknesses, and for examining the Opportunities and Threats you face.

Used in a personal context, it helps you to develop your career in a way that takes best advantage of your talents, abilities and opportunities.

What makes SWOT particularly powerful is that with a little thought, it can help you uncover opportunities that you are well placed to take advantage of. And by understanding your weaknesses, you can manage and eliminate threats that would otherwise catch your unawares.

2.3 THEORY FOR SWOT

Strengths:

- What advantages (for example, core competencies, experience, skills, education or connections) do you have that others don't have? What do you do better than anyone else?
- What personal resources do you have access to? In other words what are your personal competitive advantages amongst peers
- What do other people see as your strengths?
- What is your financial status (risk tolerance)?
- How well are you connected, i.e., Networks: personal and professional affiliations through which to make connections, contacts and garner support?

Consider this from your own perspective, and from the point of view of the people around you. And don't be modest, be as objective as you can. If you are having any difficulty with this, try writing down a list of your characteristics. Some of these will hopefully be strengths!

In looking at your strengths, think about them in relation to the people around you — for example, if you're a great mathematician and the people around you are great at math, then this is not likely to be a strength in your current role, it is likely to be a necessity.

Weaknesses:

- What could you improve?
- What should you avoid?
- What things are the people around you likely to see as weaknesses?
- What are the gaps in mission critical skills?
- Are their any gaps in competitive strength? If yes, what are those?
- Are you vulnerable to: cultural, attitudinal, behavioural aspects?
- Is location or a geography a hindrance or a weakness?

Again, consider this from a personal and external basis: Do other people perceive weaknesses that you do not see? Do co-workers consistently out-perform you in key areas? It is best to be realistic now, and face any unpleasant truths as soon as possible.

Opportunities:

A useful approach to looking at opportunities is also to look at your strengths and ask yourself whether these open up any opportunities.

- Where are the good opportunities facing you?
- What are the interesting trends you are aware of?

Useful opportunities can come from such things as:

- Changes in technology, markets and your company on both a broad and narrow scale;
- Changes in government policy related to your field;
- Changes in social patterns, population profiles, lifestyle changes, etc.; or
- Local Events
- Timely developments and trends (personal, company, industry)
- Support system(s): peers, family, personal, others
- Tactical developments, information, research and findings

Alternatively, look at your weaknesses and ask yourself whether you could open up opportunities by eliminating them.

Threats:

- What obstacles do you face?
- What are the people around you doing?
- Is your job (or the demand for the things you do) changing?
- Is changing technology threatening your position?
- Could any of your weaknesses seriously threaten you?
- Effect of corporate culture/politics
- Personal limitations and obstacles, (i.e., geography, etc.)
- Sustaining/cultivating skills through ongoing practice/education
- Anticipated/possible/likely changes to business landscape
- Insurmountable competition (peers, etc.)

Carrying out this analysis will often be illuminating — both in terms of pointing out what needs to be done, and in putting problems into perspective.

A SWOT matrix is a framework for analyzing your strengths and weaknesses, and the opportunities and threats you face. This helps you to focus on your strengths, minimize weaknesses, and take the greatest possible advantage of opportunities available.

2.4 PERSONAL SWOT ANALYSIS

After a better understanding of SWOT analysis let us first do a SWOT analysis for self. [would suggest to do a details SWOT before proceeding ahead]

Consider the overall picture of where you think you are now, and where you want to be.

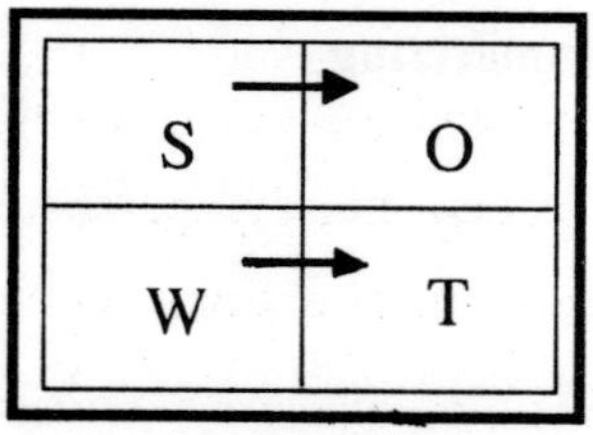

What personal skills, experience and behaviours will help you (list under strengths), and which will require some work (List under weaknesses)? What external factors (things out-weigh, your direct control) may help you (opportunities) or hinder you (threats)?

Strengths	Weakness
Opportunity	**Threat**

You can now consider how you can make the most of your strengths and opportunities, and try to develop your weaknesses and minimise your threats. This will form a key part of your personal development plan.

2.3 FEW IMPORTANT TRAITS FOR A SUCCESS IN RETAIL SALES

1. Creating a positive impression
   - Appearance
   - Approach
   - First few words
2. Communication skills
   - Listening
   - Body language
   - Paraphrasing/summarizing
   - Verbal
3. Empathy
4. Objection handling
5. Knowledge
   - Product knowledge
   - Company/Organization knowledge
   - Competition
   - Upcoming trends
6. Being Assertive
7. Managing anger

We will now just touch upon the traits mentioned above and a detailed discussion will be done in the consequent chapters as per the requirement of the context and topic.

2.3.1 Creating a positive first impression

We all have heard about 'first impression is the last impression'. But it does not end here. "First impression should be the best impression as it has to be a lasting impression." So what all matters.

(a) Appearance

(b) Approach

(c) First few words.

2.3.1 (a) Appearance

Appearance mainly defines the image that is created in the minds of consumer. Personality plays an important role in appearance which does not only mean good looks. Even if our looks do not support our appearance one can easily overcome this by the way he/she carries themselves.

Thus, grooming plays a very important role in appearance. Grooming includes:

1. ***Basic personal hygiene like:*** bathing, brushing, cleanliness, neat appearance, body-odour, etc.
2. ***Dress sense:*** although almost all the bigger retailers would have their defined dress code or a uniform, one must keep them neat and clean.

Even if a uniform is not mentioned by a retailer, one should be neatly dressed keeping in mind the socio-culture environment and the theme of the retailer also sometimes the occasion.

e.g., If it is a gaming retailer who mainly attracts young teens then the grooming should be as per the choice of the teens.

3. ***Proper footwear:*** One's footwear should always match the dress and the occasion, e.g., if a person is wearing a formal attire with a tie then only formal shoes should be accompanies with such an attire.

Many a times, people are seen giving reasons like 'shoes are shoes, how does it matter are they formal or not'. But one forgets that your grooming does not only reflect your personality. but also creates an image about your organization.

One, who has realized the virtues of good grooming, should also make graciousness a part of his or her personality. Having embraced 'grace', one should grow and travel through the journey of life with grace. One's behaviour should change with age. That is the difference between staying young at heart and acting young. For instance, coyness in a young woman is permissible but if stretched as the years roll on, it would seem like a pathetic attempt to remain 'girlish'.

A distinguished look is in effect a composition of individual elements. These are:

- Poise
- Clothes
- Fashion
- Accessories
- Jewellery
- Personal care
- Make-up
- Hair
- Dressing for the occasion

While grooming one should very .meticulously take care of the following:

- Neat appearance
- Styles that highlight your strengths and shield your drawbacks
- Fabric of clothes

- Colour co-ordination of clothes
- Appropriate accessories — ties bows, socks, belts, handkerchiefs, scarves
- Right make-up
- Hair/hairstyle
- Shoes
- Perfumes/Aftershave Lotions
- Briefcase/Handbags
- Strive for simplicity
- Jewellery must complement NOT overpower the personality of the wearer
- Do not use gaudy and flashy jewellery
- No chipped nail polish

In addition to visual appeal, each of the above brings about self-awareness, self-confidence and self-esteem. All these individual aspects need to be cultivated singly and collectively to create a complete, harmonious and pleasing picture. When one knows one looks well, one naturally feels good and exudes self-confidence.

2.3.1 (b) Approach

Approaching anybody would many times feel like appearing for an examination, as many of the people get butterflies in their stomach. While approaching anybody one needs to be confident. Remember customer expert sales guys to know what they are talking about. In contrast, absence of an adequate level of knowledge is likely to make the salesperson diffident at best. This could explain why some salespeople seem reluctant to approach customers, they are worried they might be asked a question which they cannot handle.

Approach also includes the way you walk towards the customer consider the following example:

> "You are a floor manager in an apparel section, suddenly you see women of small stature (built) say 4 feet 9" in height and very lean. You feel she is a bit confused in choosing a garment. So you decided to extend help. Thus, from the corner of the floor you start to walk towards her taking giant steps with full of confidence on your face. The lady sees you approaching her and there is a sudden fear on her face. She is just stand still with eyes wide open. You go and ask her if she requires any help. She refuses while taking a few steps back and then just walks off to the other section.

Many a times such an incident is visible in small as well as large format stores. Thus, while approaching, confidence is important but overconfidence is bad. Your aggression may score away the customer.

2.3.1 (c) First few words:

Thus, imagine a situation where you walk into a store, and as soon you enter, you are approached by a huge hefty man and he asks you in a very husky and dominant voice,

"What do you want to buy?" OR

"Do you want to buy anything?"

I am sure this will score you out of the store. Neither would you want to visit the store again nor would you recommend your friends and relatives to visit that store.

Thus, it is rightly said the first 15-20 words make or a break the future conversation. One should, thus, be very careful with the first few words. Many companies have standard opening for all of their customer facing roles.

Few points to remember

- Always smile [genuine smile]
- Be polite
- Give a feeling of 'we understand and know what you want'.

2.3.2 Communication skill

Communication skill forms a very important aspect of an successful person. Many people limit the communication skill to verbal communication, but verbal communication is just a small part of the overall communication skill. Here we would touch upon the aspect which is important with retail as a prospective. They are as follows:

(a) Listening skills

(b) Body language

(c) Paraphrasing/summarizing

(d) Verbal communication

2.3.2 (a) Listening skills

One of the most important skills for the salesperson. Often salespeople want to give the most of the information on a product, service and promotional offer to the customer. But one should listen to the customer's needs and desires to the product and the services which he/she is offering.

As it is often said, 'god gave use one mouth to speak but two ears to listen' thus, emphasizing on the importance of listening.

Listening Skills

1. Sit up.
2. Look interested.
3. Lean forward.
4. Listen.
5. Act interested.
6. Nod your head to show that you are tuned in.
7. Track the speaker with your eyes.

Listening tips:

- Stop talking. You can't listen if you're talking.
- Give positive feedback. Look and act interested. Positive head nods, alertness, and smiles — all offer encouragement to the speaker.
- Ask questions. Questions that show interest and attention encourage both speaker and listener. Show your interest.
- Empathize with the speaker. Put yourself in the speaker's place; this will help you understand the message.
- Keep confidences. If the information is sensitive, don't share it with others.
- Share information. We tend to tell things to those who tell us things. So if you want the speaker to share information with you, share information with the speaker.
- Use good posture. Sit up straight, yet comfortably. Good posture aids breathing and alertness. It also communicates positive interest to the speaker.

- Follow the speaker. If the speaker moves, turn your head or rotate in your chair to maintain eye contact and attention. This movement also aids in keeping you alert.
- Don't be a deadpan. Facial expressions, head nods, and tilts of the head show your involvement and provide positive feedback to the speaker.

2.3.2 (b) Body language

Whenever in a retail store you as a salesperson would be observed by many customers also you would be required to observe the body language of customers to see whether they

- Need any help
- Are looking for something else
- Are looking for someone
- Are sending buying signals
- Are not convinced with what they buying

You as a salesperson should always display positive and encouraging body language, e.g:

(1) Always smile. But the smile should not be a plastic smile, you should smile genuinely.

(2) Always use your hands to show directions to the customer.

(3) Keep safe distance from the customer. 25 inches surrounding every person is said to be his/her personal space. One should avoid getting into customers personal space.

Tips on body language

- **Don't cross your arms or legs –** You have probably already heard you shouldn't cross your arms as it might make you seem defensive or guarded. This goes for your legs too.
- **Have eye contact, but don't stare** – If there are several people you are talking to, give them all some eye contact to create a better connection and see if they are listening. Keeping too much eye contact might creep people out. Giving no eye contact might make you seem insecure. If you are not used to keeping eye contact it might feel a little hard or scary in the beginning but keep working on it and you'll get used to it.
- **Don't be afraid to take up some space** – Taking up space by for example sitting or standing with your legs apart a bit signals self-confidence and that you are comfortable in your own skin.
- **Relax your shoulders** – When you feel tense it is easily winds up as tension in your shoulders. They might move up and forward a bit. Try to relax. Try to loosen up by shaking the shoulders a bit and move them back slightly.
- **Nod when they are talking** – Nod once in a while to signal that you are listening. But don't overdo it and peck like woody woodpecker.
- **Lean, but not too much –** If you want to show that you are interested in what someone is saying, lean toward the person talking. If you want to show that you're confident in yourself and relaxed lean back a bit. But don't lean in too much or you might seem needy and desperate for some approval. Or lean back too much or you might seem arrogant and distant.
- **Smile and laugh** – Lighten up, don't take yourself too seriously. Relax a bit, smile and laugh when someone says something funny. People

will be a lot more inclined to listen to you, if you seem to be a positive person. But don't be the first to laugh at your own jokes, it makes you seem nervous and needy. Smile when you are introduced to someone but don't keep a smile plastered on your face, you'll seem insincere.

- **Don't touch your face** – It might make you seem nervous and can be distracting for the listeners or the people in the conversation.
- **Keep you head up** – Don't keep your eyes on the ground, it might make you seem insecure and a bit lost. Keep your head up straight and your eyes towards the horizon.
- **Slowdown a bit** – This goes for many things. Walking slower not only makes you seem more calm and confident, it will also make you feel less stressed. If someone addresses you, don't snap you're neck in their direction, turn it a bit more slowly instead.
- **Use your hands more confidently** – Instead of fidgeting with your hands and scratching your face use them to communicate what you are trying to say. Use your hands to describe something or to add weight to a point you are trying to make. But don't use them too much or it might become distracting. And don't let your hands flail around, use them with some control.
- **Realise where your spine ends** – Many people might sit or stand with a straight back in a good posture. However, they might think that the spine ends where the neck begins and therefore crane the neck forward. Your spine ends in the back of your head. Keep your whole spine straight and aligned for better posture.
- **Don't stand too close** – One of the things we learned from Seinfeld is that everybody gets weirded out by a close-talker. Let people have their personal space, don't invade it.
- **Mirror** – Often when you get along with a person, when the two of you get a good connection, you will start to mirror each other subconsciously. That means that you mirror the other person's body language a bit. To make the connection better you can try a bit of proactive mirroring. If he leans forward, you might lean forward. If she holds her hands on her thighs, you might do the same. But don't react instantly and don't mirror every change in body language. Then weirdness will ensue.

- **Keep a good attitude** – Last but not the least, keep a positive, open and relaxed attitude. How you feel will come through in your body language and can make a major difference.

2.3.2 (c) Paraphrasing/summarizing

An important quality (or skill) is that of being able to understand the customer needs and able to give a product or solution in accordance with the expressed needs and desires. But to get the understanding right it is very important to get your understanding authenticated by the customer himself. This can be effectively done by summarizing whatever customer has asked for this could be as,

(1) "Sir, just to check my understanding right this is what you want?"..........."

(2) "Please correct me if I am wrong in my understanding................"

By this both the customer and the salesperson are on the same page of understanding about the customers needs and desires.

Paraphrasing is also of very much importance, when after a purchase of a certain product, the sales person should read aloud the items present in the package. Also, many a times it is advised to re-emphasize on the guarantee and warrantee terms at the counter of sales.

2.3.2 (d) Verbal communication

As somebody has rightly said "one needs to be a Chinese in China and Indian in India." One needs to be very careful also with their verbal communication. Imagine you are a salesperson in a consumer electronic section and you get a blinds speaking client who wants to buy a washing machine. You should not give a demonstration in English; your demonstration of the product should be in Hindi. If the client's language and the salesperson's language are not in the same ground the client may feel offended.

Also verbal communication is not about only language, but a salesperson should be able to articulate his/her thoughts in a proper manner. Thus, in other words the salesperson should know

- What to say?
- When to say?
- How much to say?
- How to say?

To get your verbal communications remember the two Ws with two Hs.

But verbal communication does not limit itself to saying but it also includes asking. In other words probing the customer with the right kind of questions to get appropriate responses. Thus, the above theory also extends to a salesperson should know?

- What to ask?
- When to ask?
- How much to ask?
- How to ask?

e.g.: A customer is in the casual section of a large apparel retail store. You are seeing him holding a T-shirt in hand and a confused look on the face. You approach him:

Scene 1 :- "Can I help you"

The answer could be either on Yes or a No.

Scene 2 :- "Sir do you want to see somemore colours in that pattern".

A scene 2 type of question may lead to a further discussion, whereas scene 1 has a 50-50% chance of the conversation going forward.

Thus, depending on the situation the questions should be either close or open-ended.

2.3.3 Empathy

Empathy is defined by Wikipedia as: "the capacity to recognize or understand another's state of mind or emotion. Empathy is a way of saying "I put myself in your shoes and then think". Thus, leading to establish a constructive relationship. Empathy does not necessarily imply compassion or empathic concern because this capacity can be present in context of compassionate or cruel behaviour." Remember the customer does not want to buy anything what a salesperson wants to sell; rather the customer wants to buy what he/she wants or desires. As soon as the salesperson put himself in the customer's shoes, he/she is able to see things according to the customer's perspective and making the customer much more comfortable and helping in the buying process.

The best way to get what you want out of life is to help others get what they want. Empathy and genuine concern encourage communication. – Zig Ziglar

From this perspective on what empathy means, it is clear that it is critical for a salesperson to have or to develop a high level of empathy to have great success. Some people, will naturally be more empathetic than others, yet luckily, this is something that can be developed for those who lack a high degree of empathy.

Points to Remember
(1) Quickly read the customer's unique personality without a questionnaire.
(2) Understand why they do, what they do, which will give you a better understanding, why is the customer buying whatever he/she is buying.
(3) Then put yourself in the customer's position and think how would you like to be treated.
(4) Employ the right strategy to achieve the best result for both.

2.3.4 Objection handling

As salespeople objections are a part of daily life. A customer has every right to get his/her doubts cleared before buying a product or a service. This clearance of doubts comes in front of a salesperson as objections.

Objection statements could be as:

- **Objection on product/service**
  - I don't like this feature.
  - The colour is too dull
  - Product does not support my requirement
  - Service centre is too far
- **Objection on price**
  - This seems to be very expensive
- **Other objections**
  - Next time I will come with my wife, she is the one who will use this [Authority objection]
  - I do not require it now
  - I do not trust this brand [Brand objection]

As a salesperson one needs to take these objections in a positive manner and handle all of them in very persuasive manner.

A salesperson should beforehand be prepared with all the possible objections he/she might come across. This will give the salesperson a great amount of confidence in handling objections. Even after preparation if a salesperson comes across an objection which he/she is not able to handle, then he/she should not try to bluff. Rather than bluffing, they should stick to their honesty and sincerely accept in front of the customer and involve somebody who could handle that particular objection better.

Thus, a salesperson needs to work hard to overcome the objection and a positive attitude clubbed along with sincerity will enable him/her get the sales.

2.3.5 Knowledge

Knowledge is the sum of all information known by a person. This knowledge could be acquired by many means either through internet, reading books, talking to peers, colleagues, friends, attending seminars, reading newspaper, through induction programmes, reading brochures, etc.,

For salesperson we have classified knowledge into four types, i.e.:

(a) Products

(b) Company/Organization

(c) Competition

(d) Upcoming trends

2.3.5 (a) Product knowledge

It is very important for a salesperson to know very well all the products which he/she is selling. A salesperson should take extra efforts and read the product brochures also, if possible, find out more about the product from the internet. As the customers now-a-days have a access to a lot of information, thus, they might ask a salesperson some technical or an in-depth questions about the product. If the salesperson is able to handle the query/objection properly then this will also form a brand of the company.

2.3.5 (b) Company/organization knowledge

One should know about the organization he or she is working for, e.g., you are working for a large retailer who has their presence in supermarkets, hypermarkets as well as in speciality stores. You are located in a speciality store which deals with music and sound systems. One day you get a customer who wants to buy a high-end hometheatre, which you have convincingly sold to him. Along with the system you have given him a gift voucher of Rs. 5,000/- which is redeemable in the supermarket. So, now it is your duty to explain the client about the details of the supermarket.

Thus, you should know all the details of your company which would be handled during the induction programme. But apart from that one should always keep themselves updated on the current happenings in the company in – reading or browsing.

2.3.5 (c) Competition

For example, you are working with a food retailer in the loose pulses section, and then in that case you should know at what price other retailers in your area are selling the same pulse. If you know this then you can use this information in your advantage for increasing sales.

A salesperson should always keeps the information of competitors.

2.3.5 (d) Up-coming trends

As mentioned in the earlier section now-a-days customers are very well aware of the trends and newer products and services available. Thus, to gain trust and seem knowledgeable one updated with the current trends a salesperson should always keep him/herself updated with the upcoming trends in your respective line of business.

2.3.6 Being assertive

Assertiveness is a positive self-expression that conveys self-confidence. Utmost care should be taken while being assertive as many a times the customer might feel as if the salesperson is being dominant or pushy in approach.

Assertive thinking, involves concern for one's own welfare and goal with an active concern for the welfare and goals of others. It also like expressing willingness to probe more deeply into the motives of one's self and others. Being assertive basically means standing up for expressing thoughts, feelings in a direct, honest and appropriate way which does not — another persons rights or kills the other persons needs.

In short it is a win-win solution

Characteristics of Assertive Behaviour:

(1) Self-confidence and high self-esteem

(2) Respect for self and others

(3) Take responsibility

(4) Concerned about others feelings and thoughts

(5) Ask opinions and listens

(6) Honest and Direct

(7) Ask others for feedback

Skills of Assertions:

(1) Give information

(2) Give your opinion or point of view

(3) Be direct without biases

(4) Be descriptive

(5) Stick to your point of view.

2.3.7 Managing anger

All customers are not the same. There would be some customers who sometimes might get on to your nerves. We all have read, studied and believed 'Customer is the king' but we too are human beings, thus, emotions are a part and parcel. So there are choices of us also being angry. So how do we manage this.

First let us understand anger. Anger is an emotional state that worries in intensity from mild irritation to intense fury and rage. Normal anger is said to be good to maintain healthy human emotions. But is dysfunctional when gets out of control and turns destructive.

Job Description for SM/ASM/CSS

For SM (Store Manager)/ASM (Assistant Store Manager):-

- Understanding the strategic plan of the organisation
- Achieving and exceeding the targets set for the store on agreed variables (sales, margins, sales per sq. ft., stock turns, etc. and working towards reducing costs and other administrative expenses).
- Monitoring the day-to-day store operations as per defined process/policy.
- Co-ordinating with the logistics team to understand ensure product availability, stocks and global count.
- Maintaining appropriate level of stocks in the store to serve customers properly.
- To make sure the property under his/her supervision is properly maintained and always presentable

- Managing of cash pickups
- Overseeing store opening and closing on time (briefing and debriefing staff)
- Float cash management
- Ensure 100% compliance to planogram, Visual Merchandising and Merchandising plan
- Order management and responsible for store fill
- Taking charge of store staff training and implementing it on regular basis.
- Achieving the defined level of customer service in the store.
- Continuously communicating with all store staff; maintaining high performance and team culture of the organisation.
- Liaisons with various external authorities for ensuring all statutory and mandatory requirements are met with.
- To ensure all customer feedback/complaints are satisfactorily handled

Desired profile and competencies

- SM: Graduate 5 + years of experience, exposure to retail environment will be an added advantage.
- ASM: Undergraduate 4 + years of experience, exposure to retail environment will be an added advantage.

Functional

- High degree of customer orientation
- Excellent selling and communication skills
- Proficiency in Hindi and/or English and one local language
- Process orientation and product/industry knowledge
- Capacity to learn new skills
- Basic working knowledge of computers

2.4 SUMMARY

It is very important for a person to understand their strenghts and weakness and which will in turn help them to work on the same. For this, a person should use a SWOT analysis for himself, even if it takes a but of time it is fine but this will help a person in shopping his/her future. Also every profession requires some or the other traits, one should map them, his/her SWOT to the requirements of that particular profession. Thereby will be able to find where he/she stands. Thus, one will also know where he/she requires improvement. Similarly, retail sales also requires some traits which should match your strengths to become a successful retail sales professional.

2.8 SELF ASSESSMENT QUESTIONS

1. Do a detailed SWOT analysis for at least two large retailers in your city.
2. Do a detailed SWOT analysis for yourself and map it with the traits required for a sales person.
3. Explain the importance of creating a positive first impression.

3 Chapter

CUSTOMER IDENTIFICATION AND APPROACH

Objectives

After going through this chapter, you will be able to understand:

- Different types of customers
- How to identify a customer
- Some basic tips on body language
- How to grasp customers attention
- The methods to approach the customer

Structure:

3.1 Customer Identification

3.1.1 Customer 1: THE LOYAL CUSTOMER

3.1.2 Customer 2: THE FICKLE CUSTOMER

3.1.3 Customer 3: THE RENEWING CUSTOMER

3.1.4 Customer 4: THE NEW CUSTOMER

3.2 Physical Appearance

3.3 Body Language

3.4 Grasping Customer's Attention

3.4.1 Importance of customer

3.4.2 Importance of merchandise

3.4.3 Importance of people

3.5 Customer Approach

3.5.1 Objective of the approach

3.5.2 Timing of approach

3.5.3 Types of approach:

3.5.4 Common mistakes in approaching

3.6 Summary

3.7 Self Assessment Questions

The very reason for not only success but also existence of every business is 'The Customer'. IT is the customer who can make or break the business. All these things we have been hearing for ages, but the question is:

- How does one identify on customer
- How to grasp the attention of a customer
- How to also handle the customer.

These are exactly the things which we will discuss in this chapter.

3.1 CUSTOMER IDENTIFICATION

Many a times you hear people saying "I can identify a person by just looking at him/her".

OR

"Just a glance and I know the required things absent the person".

But unfortunately god has not gifted everyone with such senses. Also, it is very dangerous to judge a person on his/her appearance or the way they speak. On the contrary people who love to show off may be well dressed and want to create an impression which could be false *Vis-a-versa* people who have a higher disposable income would not like to make their presence loud:

I'd like you to think about your "sales world" as one that is made up of four kinds of customers—Loyal, Fickle, Renewing and New. And the strategies you use to convert them to customers are different for each.

Let us go through each one of them in detail

3.1.1 Customer 1: THE LOYAL CUSTOMER

LOYAL CUSTOMERS are those who will always invite you to work with them to solve a problem and will negotiate with you to provide the products and services they need. They continue to do business with you day-after-day because they appreciate the unique skills or products you have and you add value to their business. They would visit your store whenever they require anything, many a times they might be aware that you might not have that product but would like to take your opinion regarding the same from where do they buy what they require.

Selling strategy for LOYAL CUSTOMERS:

(1) Continue offering them high value products and services that add value to them.

(2) Communicate often with them to evaluate your effectiveness and their opinion of you.

(3) When "moments of misery" happen, immediately commit all necessary resources to fixing the problem.

3.1.2 Customer 2: THE FICKLE CUSTOMER

Many people try to avoid FICKLE CUSTOMERS because they can be the most difficult to work with. They usually ask for a price on a product and also all the possible freebies attached to it but will then shop around for the "best deal." They may actually be loyal customers of one of your competitors and only by looking and assuring themselves that they are getting the best deals (from your competitors) either way, they can waste your time.

Yet, FICKLE CUSTOMERS are potential loyal customers. Even their round to various stores checking out the best prices and the freebies can be converted to loyal customers. Here's how:

Selling strategy for FICKLE CUSTOMERS:

(1) First, you need to identify what they like about their current preferred vendor and what they don't like about that vendor.

(2) Then create a plan that will gain their trust and loyalty. In a positive way, show how you are better than their current vendor. Consider using testimonials from current clients to help push the scales your way.

(3) Be sure to explain this strategy to all those involved in making this FICKLE CUSTOMER into a loyal one.

Here I would like to share an example of my friend. Whenever he wants to buy grocery his preferred store is Food Bazzar, but he will make a point to visit the 'Star Bazzar' as well as the Hypercity which are both close to his house. Just a couple months back when carrying out his activity of price hunting religiously, he came across a salesperson at Star Bazzar. Once he was out of Star Bazzar he had not only bought the monthly grocery from their but also started recommending the store to others.

Thus, if once you are able to convert these fickle customers into your customers, they end up being very loyal customers and also get some more loyal customers along with them.

3.1.3 Customer 3: THE RENEWING CUSTOMER

RENEWING CUSTOMERS are those that used to do a significant business with you but have for some reason slipped away. In a store you will many a times come across some customers who use to regularly visit the store and buy a lot of stuff, but off late you do not find them in the store so often. They have given you good business in the past and have the potential to return to previous levels. The reason could be they are coming across some other store from where they do their buying and just a very minuscule part comes to your store, as occasionally they come to check prices and in the process pick up some stuff just for name sake.

RENEWING CUSTOMERS require a similar strategy to both fickle and new. Here's how you them back:

Selling strategy for RENEWING CUSTOMERS:

(1) First, identify the root cause of their drifting away to the competition.

(2) Then determine whether you can earn their loyalty again.

(3) Next, make and execute a plan that will regain their confidence in you, which could mean show them the value of buying from your store.

(4) Finally, you'll need to explain the what, how and why to everyone on your "customer recovery team."

3.1.4 Customer 4: THE NEW CUSTOMER

NEW CUSTOMERS are the people whom you have been seeing for the first time, or there could be some people who would approach you and enquire about the utilities availability like electricity bill counters, telephone exchange location or good restaurants. They might also many times directly mention that they have recently shifted to this location. These target customers look and act like your best loyal customers. They usually have many similarities, including social status, location, cultural background, and so on. The more you know about these NEW CUSTOMERS, the better chance you have to convert them in to loyal customers.

Selling strategy for NEW CUSTOMERS:

(1) To add a new customer, the first step is to identify the people as the new customers

(2) Gather as much as information as possible from them, about them.

(3) Next you'll have to inform them of your capabilities and persuade them to offer your product or services.

(4) After that you'll need to nurture them into becoming loyal customers by providing the very best service and products that exceed their expectations.

Remember "make every contact with your customers a 'moment of magic' instead of a 'moment of misery". Then you'll be well on your way to earning and keeping good customers.

3.2 PHYSICAL APPEARANCE

There is this old saying, 'Never judge a book by its cover'. A few years ago I came across this fact and would like to share the same with you to sensitize the importance of physical appearance.

"A lady in a faded grey dress and her husband, dressed in a homespun suit walked in timidly without an appointment into the Harvard University President's outer office.

The secretary could tell in a moment that such backwoods, country hicks had no business at Harvard and probably didn't even deserve to be in Harvard.

'We want to see the President,' the man said softly. 'He'll be busy all day,' the secretary snapped. 'We'll wait,' the lady replied.

For hours the secretary ignored them, hoping that the couple would finally become discouraged and go away.

They didn't and the secretary grew frustrated and finally decided to disturb the president. 'Maybe if you see them for a few minutes, they'll leave,' she said to him.

The President, stern faced and with dignity, strutted towards the couple.

The lady told him, 'We had a son who attended Harvard for one year. He loved Harvard. He was happy here. But about a year ago, he was accidentally killed.

My husband and I would like to erect a memorial to him, somewhere on 'campus.' The president wasn't touched....

He was shocked. 'Madam,' he said, gruffly, 'we can't put up a statue for every person who attended Harvard and died. If we did, this place would look like a cemetery.

'Oh, no,' the lady explained quickly. 'We don't want to erect a statue. We thought we would like to give a building to Harvard.'

The president rolled his eyes. He glanced at the gingham dress and homespun suit, and then exclaimed, 'A building!'

Do you have any earthly idea how much a building costs? We have over seven and a half million dollars in the physical buildings here at Harvard.

' For a moment the lady was silent. The president was pleased. Maybe he! could get rid of them now.

The lady turned to her husband and said quietly, 'Is that all it costs to start a university? Why don't we just start our own?'

Her husband nodded.

The president's face wilted in confusion and bewilderment.

Mr. and Mrs. Leland Stanford got up and walked away, travelling to Palo Alto, California where they established the University that bears their name? Stanford University, a memorial to a son that Harvard no longer cared about.

Most of the time we judge people by their outer appearance, which can be misleading. And in this impression only we tend to treat people badly by thinking they can do nothing for us thus we tend to lose our potential customers. One should be very careful while judging a person based on the appearance.

On the contrary to the above mentioned example of 'Stanford', one could come across a customer who is very well dressed and also comes across very neatly but might end up to be a shop-lifter.

Foul play by the fair sex

15 Jul 2004, 0309 hrs IST, Manjari Sabharwal, TNN

Print Email Discuss Share Save Comment Text:

When it comes to shop lifting women are on the prowl in a big way here in Kanpur.

Sample this: Items worth Rs 10,000 stolen from a departmental store. Guilty- two ladies who were caught but released by shop owners in order to maintain goodwill amongst customers.

Manoj Mehrotra, a cloth merchant in Gumti says, "Recently a well dressed lady, wearing lots of jewellery and carrying 2-3 handbags came to my shop and while I was attending to other customers, quietly put two cloth pieces into her bag and started moving out. That very moment my servant caught her and reported the matter to me. I was shocked to see how ladies who appear to belong to good families can do such things. I took the cloth pieces back and let her go. I obviously could not do anything as she started crying and begging to spare her."

Briefing on the modus operandi of women shop lifters, Suraj Singh, the owner of a departmental store says, "The women shop lifters generally carry 2-3 handbags and are well dressed so that no one can guage their intentions. At times they wear the burqa so that they can cover their faces and can steal better and more easily. A couple of weeks back two such ladies stole cosmetics worth Rs 10,000, but we caught them and took the things back."

Source: http://timesofindia.indiatimes.com/articleshow/778767.cms

One should be very careful while judging a person based on his/her looks. Many a times we have a perception and biases based on our past experiences. This could also lead to forming opinions about a particular person, community or a region. But one should always remember that everyone cannot be characterized into a pool and be concluded.

3.3 BODY LANGUAGE

Body language (those gestures, body movements, facial expressions and other forms of non-verbal behaviour) serves as a mirror to our inner thoughts. As children and young adults, we learned how to control our words. We quickly learned what we could say that would be acceptable to those around us. We even learned how to say it. We consciously worked and re-worked our words to make sure we said what we meant to say.

Body language can be categorized into following groups:

(1) Posture

(2) Limbs Movement

(3) Eye contact

(4) Facial Expression

Many a times we also are able to read the body language but the question is what do we do next?

Most of the times there are three simple responses that will work.

1. Stop what you are saying or doing and ASK THEM A QUESTION.
2. Trial close. (Try to close the deal)
3. Offer empathy. "You look like you have a question?" You seem concerned" "You look interested".

According to one of the international personality Evancar Michael the following are some of the signals which could be looked for:

Customer eyes	
Starring	Indicate a need for the customer to control you and the meeting.
Avioding eye contact	They are uncomfortable with you, or trying to hide something from you.
Sparkle or Glint	They are having fun – maybe even getting excited about your solution
Glassy-eyed	Bored.
Looking up and to the side	Recalling something, or imagining something – maybe how your solution will work for them
Looking sideways	Recalling something they heard
Casting their eyes down	Experiencing an unpleasant emotion
Shifting eyes	Lying or looking for a way out
Glancing towards an object	They want to talk about it in the room, a brochure, sample
The Customer's Hands	
Drumming their fingers	Impatience, "get to the point"
Playing with a pen or pencil, shuffling papers	Concerned, annoyed, confused or wanting to say something
Pointing at you, jabbing the desk with their finger	Angry or frustrated
One hand holding the other wrist down	on guard, threatened or very cautious

Touching, picking up or caressing your product	Major Buying signal
Folded across the chest	usually means they are protecting information or feelings
Hands lightly crossed or open, resting on the desk	Interested, trusting
Face	
Lightly rubbing the side	lying or at least, not sure of the veracity of what they are of the nose with a finger telling you when talking
Stroking the chin	reflecting on what you are saying
Posture	
Leaning back	wanting to distancing themselves from you or your proposal
Leaning forward	interested
Bolt upright, stiff	need for control, seeking deference from you

As discussed earlier we rehearse what to say many a times in our mind and sometimes also in practice. But how many times do we rehearse our body language? The answer is very few times. Similarly, majority of the customers fall in the unrehearsed body language category, thus making the job of the sales person easier to read between the lines and understand the hidden message.

In retail store one should always remember that the customers need to be given time and space — especially around the merchandise. Positive customers who have a definite purchase in mind will probably show their feelings by making a direct approach to the salesperson. Others who are looking for information about their potential purchases and the salesperson is too positive, the customer might think the salesperson is getting too pushy. So, it is important not to crowd the customer.

Although the body language is not quite a scientific as it might appear. We are often taught and also many times told that if the person does not establish proper eye contact he/she is not confident. But this necessarily not right always. May be the person has some medical problem or he is shy in nature. There could be any reason, but one cannot reach a conclusion based on this. A salesperson requires to take a holistic approach.

3.4 GRASPING CUSTOMER'S ATTENTION

There could be number of ways by which customer's attention could be grasped. Many a times the attention could be grasped while the customer is passing by the entrance at the store. It could also be through a marketing or a promotional campaign which could vary from a simple hoarding or a pamphlet or a big budget advertisement aired during the prime time. Unless the customer has made a conscious decision to visit the store, all the above mentioned activities play on vital role in grasping a customer's attention.

Some of the external factors just outside the store which help in grasping customer's attentions are as follows:

(1) Merchandise collections

(2) Display's at the entrance

(3) Promotion (i.e., discounts, freebies, display ads)

(4) Lighting

(5) Mannequins/fixtures (if any)

(6) Sign board

(7) Atmosphere and the environment surrounding the store (e.g. cleanliness, tidiness, location, decor, etc.)

These all factors part an very important part of the external trading environment.

The internal environment basically is formed of 3 important elements which are as follows:

(1) The customer

(2) The merchandise

(3) The people (employees, salespeople, etc.)

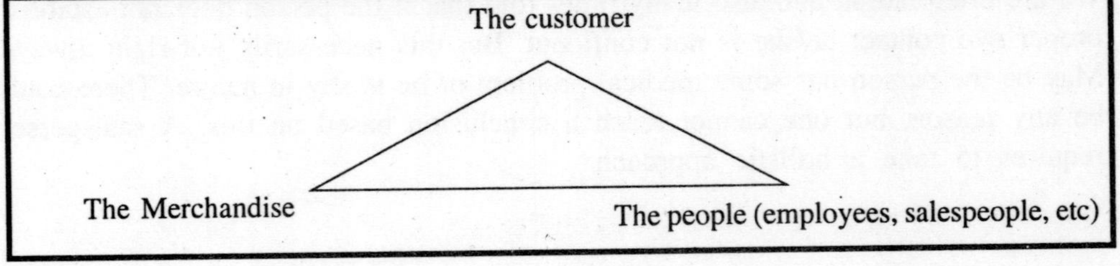

3.4.1 Importance of customer

As we have been discussing right from the beginning customer is the very reason for our existence. Below given are few points to re-emphasize the importance of the customer:

(1) Customer is the source of all sales and profit.

(2) We are dependant on the customer for growth and expansion of the company.

(3) Customer pays our salary

(4) Customer is not only an asset but also an asset which appreciates in value.

(5) Customer is a marketing tool and a source of free advertisement.

(6) The retail business revolves around how well a retailer understands the customer and their respective needs.

3.4.2 Importance of merchandise

Today the customer is pampered with choices. So, slowly the customer is getting habituated to look for options from where he/she can choose from. Thus, in such a scenario merchandise plays a very very important role. Following are the few points to touch the importance at merchandise:

(1) Merchandise is one of the important reasons, why customer comes to store.

(2) Quality of merchandise builds loyalty.

(3) Quality as well as range of the merchandise represents the image of the retailer/store.

(4) For the customer, the way the merchandise is laid out becomes on important part of his/her shopping experience.

(5) Range of merchandise increases the buying and thus, leads to sales and profitability.

3.4.3 Importance of people

People form a very important part of any business. In a store the customer might be coming to buy a product, but will interact with people in the store. Thus, not only people in the customer facing roles but also the hockend people form a very important role in grasping the customer attention. It is the salesperson who will project the image of the product/service in the front of the customer. Thus, to highlight the importance of people let us consider the following points:

(1) Human contact increases the livelihood of the sale.

(2) The salesperson plays a vital role in persuading information and building the confidence to purchase.

(3) Buying decisions in retail are often made within a store, thus, a conducive and a sales enhancing environment built by people surely increases sales.

(4) The salesperson plays a critical role in relationship building and making loyal customers.

3.5 CUSTOMER APPROACH

At this stage after identifying the customer and grasping the customers attention the salesperson needs to approach the customer. But before approaching give a thought over the thought process in the customer's mind regarding you. He could be thinking any of the following:

"I would like to be welcomed"

"I am important and would like to be acknowledged"

"Consider my needs and help me find what I am looking for"

"How will you help me?"

These could some of the indicative thoughts in the mind of the customer. So, if these are the thoughts a salesperson approach should also be based to address the thoughts in the mind of the customer.

3.5.1 Objective of the approach

Even before approaching one should always remember the objective of approaching the customer from the customer's point of view. Thus, approach and greeting is to:

- Make the customer feel welcome
- Show the customer you are available to help him/her
- Direct the interest of the customer to the merchandise
- Make the customer feel comfortable

- Begin a relationship that will end in a sale/ service once the objective is clear then and then only the approach would be a successful approach.

3.5.2 Timing of approach

As we all know that to the things right appropriate timing is of utmost importance, the same applies in the case of approaching the customer as well. One should be very careful while approaching a customer as if the timing is wrong it might even scare away the customer or the get the customer annoyed.

Many a times, in the store a salesperson is not able to decide when to approach the customer, below given are some guidelines to help in deciding when to approach:

- Give the customer sometime to get used to the store environment and the ambience
- If greeted too soon, the customer has had no time to see the merchandise, and she feels "pounced" upon
- Too late, the customer may decide not to buy, and you lose the opportunity.
- Observe the customer to find out WHEN is the right time

As human beings let us accept that everybody wants their own privacy and the same should be respected of the customer as well. Thus, the salesperson should be able to judge whether the customer needs attention now or wants to be left alone in his or her privacy zone.

Based on this below mentioned are few tips as for when is the right time:

- When the customer feels the merchandise
- Customer looks at a price tag
- Customer spends more time on a particular section
- Customer hands are full
- Customer needs help, e.g., with a baby
- Customer looks around and tries to catch the eye of salesperson

3.5.3 Types of approach:

For simplification purpose the types of approach have classified into six types which are as follows:

(a) Non-verbal

(b) Social Greeting/Conversational Approach

(c) Merchandise greeting

(d) Special feature approach

(e) Customer Benefit Approach

(f) Compliment Approach

3.5.3 (a) Non-verbal:

As studied previously non-verbal communication includes a lot of things like body language, eye contact, gesture, posture, poise, etc.

Everybody like to see a smiling face, the same applies to the customers as well. Thus, some of the non-verbal signs of approach could be:

(i) Warm smile

(ii) Eye contact

(iii) 'May I help you' look on the face

(iv) Acknowledge the customer with a nod

3.5.3 (b) Social greeting/conversational approach

Some of the examples of social greeting are as given below:

(i) Hello, Good Morning, Good afternoon, namaste,

(ii) Hello, how may I help you,

(iii) Hello my name is Sunit…and I am here to assist you

3.5.3 (c) Merchandise greeting

Merchandise greeting is basically greeting the customer who is having a look at the merchandise. Some examples approaching a customer who is having a look at the merchandise are as follows:

(i) Good evening madam, you are looking at our new range

(ii) Are you looking for a size 40

(iii) That madam, is a colour that would suit a darker wall background

(iv) Are you looking for evening or party wear?

(v) This pattern comes in seven different colours

3.5.3 (d) Special feature approach

This could either relate to a special feature related to the product or even a promotional activity which is currently running. on that particular product. Some of the example are as follows:

(i) Ma'am, if you buy this T-shirt, you are eligible for a Special Gift Coupon

(ii) Hello Sir, there is a 30% discount on that range you are looking at

(iii) Hello, there is a special scheme on in the Accessories and Bed Linen section today

(iv) Sir, there is an offer of buy one get one free on this particular range of shoes

3.5.3 (e) Customer benefit approach

Generally the salesperson will open the conversation with the benefit statements. Thus, pointing the benefits what the customer will gain. Some example of customer benefit approach are as given below:

(i) If you buy from this section, which is the Mix'N'Match section, you can match one salwar with two or more kurtas.

(ii) However, ever many times you wash this sweater, it will not get out of shape.

(iii) In our new Designer Section, you will get designer clothes at an affordable price

3.5.3 (f) Compliment approach

Every human being like to be appreciated and giving a compliment is one of the ways to appreciate the choice of the customer. Some of the examples of compliment approach are as follows:

(i) Madam, that is also one of my favourite pieces in this section

(ii) Blue looks good on you, it suits your fair complexion

(iii) Madam, I really do like that style

(iv) See the fall of this salwar and the drape, almost as if it is made for you

3.5.4 Common mistakes in approaching

After looking at the various approaches, one should also know what kind of common mistakes a salesperson might unknowingly end up with. Some of the common mistakes made by the salesperson are as mentioned below:

(i) Too soon: not giving the customer enough time to settle

(ii) No eye contact with customer

(iii) Insincere and false compliments

(iv) Making over-smart remarks

(v) Talking too softly, too loudly, or too much

(vi) Not giving the other person your full attention

(vii) No smile

We are always taught the one should approach the customer by mentioning "May I help you", but one needs to be very careful while using this. As this might carry the following risk:

(i) Cuts off further contact if the customer says 'No',

(ii) Implies that the customer is feeling helpless and needs help,

(iii) Customer might be thinking and wants to be left alone.

3.6 SUMMARY

Many times in a retail mainly in the large format layouts people come for the experience rather than buying anything. At this point, it becomes very important for the salesperson as to not generalise everybody and recognize the right customer. For this, he/she should be aware of how to handle different types of customers and also approach them in an appropriate manner. It is also very important for the saleperson to grasp the customer's attention in a positive manner.

3.7 SELF ASSESSMENT QUESTIONS

1. Explain the difference between a 'Loyal customer' and 'Renewing customer'.
2. Write a note on different strategies to be used for different types of customer.
3. How should a salesperson gain the customer's attention?
4. Explain the different types of customer approach.
5. List down some of the common mistakes while approaching the customer.

4 Chapter

CUSTOMER NEEDS IDENTIFICATION

Objectives

After going through this chapter, you will be able to understand:

- What are the different types of consumer purchase decision.
- What are the various types of purchases.
- The various factors influencing the consumer buying behaviour.
- What motivates the customer for buying a certain product and service.
- The process of consumer buying.

Structure:

4.1 Introduction

4.2 Consumer Purchase Decisions

4.2.1 Types of consumer purchase decisions

4.3 Factors influencing the customers buying behaviour

4.3.1 Internal influences

4.3.2 External influences

4.4 Motivation for the Customer

4.5 How Consumers Buy?

4.6 Summary

4.7 Self Assessment Questions

4.1 INTRODUCTION

Many a times, salespeople wonder how some salespeople are very successful whereas some barely manage to get their sales done. As many people fail to understand sales does not only mean greeting customers, taking money, wrapping the goods. Selling involves many things beyond the normal routine transaction. Infact in some of the sections of a store, customer expects assistance from a knowledgeable person and also many times his or her decisions are based on the advice and recommendation of the salesperson. But to do so, one needs to understand the customer's needs and requirements. In short to make the customer buy one needs to first, find out what they really want, and then, show them how to get it?

The biggest question is how does one understand the customer's needs and requirements? This cannot be done by accident. This is what we will cover in this chapter. It is not only important for a salesperson to understand the customers_ needs, but using this information, marketers can create marketing programmes that they believe will be of interest to customers. As you might guess, factors affecting how customers make decisions are extremely complex. Buyer behaviour is deeply rooted in psychology with dashes of sociology thrown in just to make things more interesting. Since everyperson in the world is different, it is impossible to have simple rules that explain how buying decisions are made. Thus, we would also discuss the customer motivation and also touch upon the consumer buying behaviour in this chapter.

Below given is an experience shred by one of the customers of Vijay Sales on mouthshut.com

"Hi i am going to share my experience with regards to Vijay Sales Thane, Spacious and Variety are the two words that pop into my mind the moment someone mentions the Vijay Sales, Thane.

Vijay Sales store here has a wide variety of brands like Samsung, LG, Sony, Faber, and Dell Apple to name a few. These brands range from the latest fashion and trends in the market.

Vijay Sales, people were really customer-oriented they were very gracious, helpful polite and most important had complete knowledge of all products. They were not seems to bias for any of the product which I felt case in Croma.

I visited them twice before making final purchase and all of the time they have welcomed with deep customer care

Appearance and staff was excellent.

Branch manager had deep empathy for customer and brand name.

A truly wonderful shopping experience.

Three Cheers to Vijay Sales Thane"

vijay sales
THE No.1 FOR THE WIDEST CHOICE

4.2 CONSUMER PURCHASE DECISIONS

Not only for marketers but also to a salesperson it is important to understand how consumers treat the purchase decisions they face. If a company is targeting customers who feel a purchase decision is difficult, their marketing strategy may vary greatly from a company targeting customers who view the purchase decision as routine. Also the salesperson deployed for different type of purchase decisions made by the customer. In fact, the same company or even the same salesperson may face both situations at the same time; for some the product is new, while other customers see the purchase as routine. The implication of buying behaviour for a sales person is that different buying situations require different selling efforts and different selling approach.

4.2.1 Types of Consumer Purchase Decisions

We should also remember that the consumers are faced with purchase decisions nearly everyday. But not all decisions are treated the same. Some decisions are more complex than others and thus require more effort by the consumer. Other decisions are fairly routine and require little effort. In general, consumers face four types of purchase decisions:

(a) **Minor New Purchase:** Minor New Purchases represent something new to a consumer but in the customer's mind is not a very important purchase in terms of need, money or other reason, (e.g., status within a group).

(b) **Minor Re-Purchase:** Minor Re-Purchase are the most routine of all purchases and often the consumer returns to purchase the same product without giving much thought to other product options, (i.e., consumer is brand loyalty).

(c) **Major New Purchase:** Major New Purchases are the most difficult of all purchases because the product being purchased is important to the consumer but the consumer has little or no previous experience making these decisions. The consumer's lack of confidence in making this type of decision often (but not always) requires the consumer to engage in an extensive decision-making process.

(d) **Major Re-Purchase:** Major Re-Purchase decisions are also important to the consumer but the consumer feels confident in making these decisions since they have previous experience purchasing the product.

4.3 FACTORS INFLUENCING THE CUSTOMERS BUYING BEHAVIOUR

In the previous chapter we have touched upon the internal and external factors which influence the customers buying behaviour. Now here we will discuss in detail the various internal, as well as external factors influencing the customers buying behaviour.

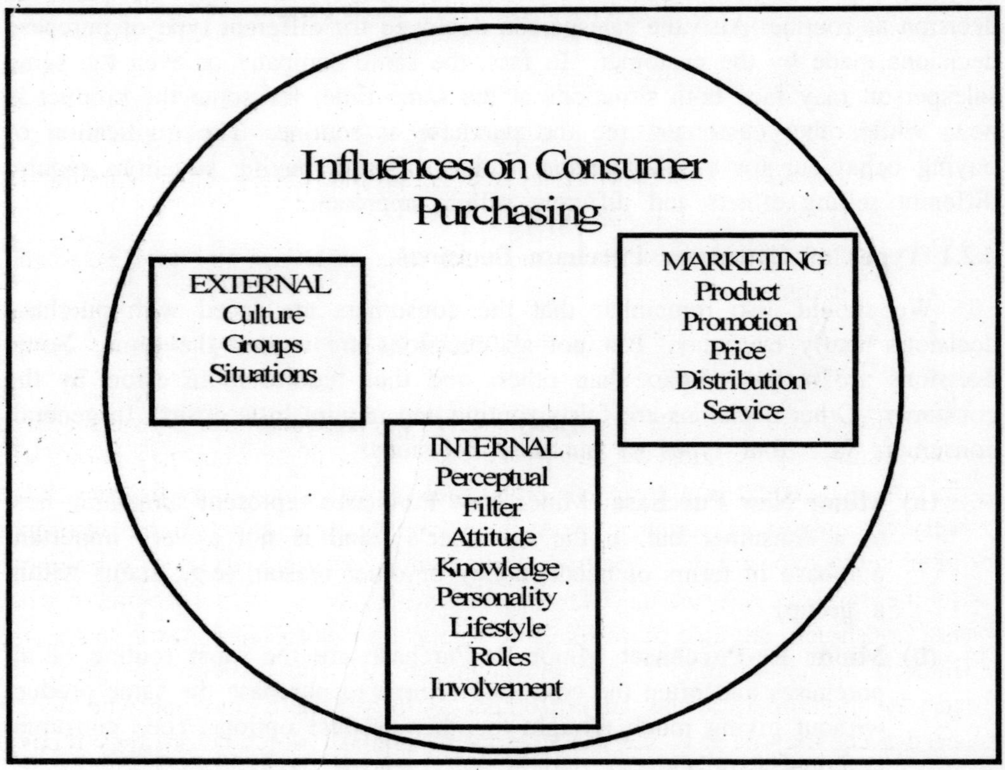

4.3.1 Internal influences

We start our examination of the influences on customer's purchase decisions by first looking inside ourselves. This will help us to identify to see most important internal factors that affect the way we make choices.

4.3.1 (a) Perceptual Filter

Perception is how we see ourselves and the world we live in. The perception which we could have formed over a period of time. This could be due to number of reasons such as the social environment in which we are brought up, or a past experience which we or any of the person whom we know has had it, or it could also be an effect from the kind of books or magazines which we read.

However, what ends up being stored inside us doesn't always get there in a direct manner. Often our mental makeup results from information that has been consciously or subconsciously filtered as we experience it, a process we refer to as a perceptual filter. To us this is our reality, though it does not mean it is an accurate reflection on what is real. Thus, perception is the way we filter stimuli, (e.g., someone talking to us, reading a newspaper story) and then make sense out of it.

Perception has several steps:

- ***Exposure*** – sensing a stimuli, (e.g., seeing an ad)
- ***Attention*** – an effort to recognize the nature of a stimuli, (e.g., recognizing it is an ad)
- ***Awareness*** – assigning meaning to a stimuli, (e.g., humorous ad for particular product)
- ***Retention*** – adding the meaning to one's internal makeup, (i.e., product has fun ads)

How these steps are eventually carried out depends on a person's approach to learning. By learning we mean how someone changes what they know, which in turn may affect how they act. For instance, one person may be able to focus very strongly on a certain advertisement and be able to retain the information after being exposed only onetime while another person may need to be exposed to the same advertisement many times before he/she even recognizes what it is. Consumers are also more likely to retain information if a person has a strong interest in the stimuli. If a person is in need of new car they are more likely to pay attention to a new advertisement for a car while someone who does not need a car may need to see the advertisement many times before they recognize the brand of automobile.

Organizations spend large sums of money in an attempt to get customers to have a positive impression of their products. But clearly the existence of a perceptual filter suggests that getting to this stage is not easy. Once the message reaches consumer it must be interesting enough to capture their attention, (e.g., talk about the product's benefits). But attending to the message is not enough. This can often happen due in part to competitive activity, (e.g., comparison advertisements). That is the reason we have been insisting on a sales-person to know the competitor products and the services the competitor is offering. Finally,. getting the consumer to give positive meaning to the message they have retained requires the retailer as well as the salesperson make sure that consumers accurately interpret the facts about the product or a service which is being offered..

4.3.1 (b) Knowledge

Knowledge is the sum of all information known by a person. In today's world we all are aware information is available free as well as in plethora. The customer has to just ask for it and he/she will have the world of information. Now it depends on the customer how well does he use this information?

I am sure you yourself must have come across many people who before buying anything would like to do an extensive research on the same (especially if it is a major buying decision). The research could be going on to the internet and finding or speaking some friends and relatives or it could even be window shopping.

It is the facts of the world as he/she knows it and the depth of knowledge is a function of the breadth of worldly experiences and the strength of an individual's long-term memory. Obviously what exists as knowledge to an individual depends on how an individual's perceptual filter makes sense of the information it is exposed to.

Many organization conduct research that will gauge consumers' level of knowledge regarding their product. Also as a sales person one should be able to gauge the level of knowledge the customer carries for the product or service. This will help in a great way for the salesperson in speaking on the same platform with the customer. To give you an example many a times you will find the salesperson trying to tell the customer the absolute basic things of the product, whereas the customer is aware about all those basic things, this might irritate the customer and create a frustration. In such a situation the customer may feel that the salesperson is underestimating his level of understand and knowledge. But on the contrary a salesperson may come across the customer who does not know anything about the product or the service and the salesperson is throwing big jargons and using technical terminologies for explanation. This might get the customer feel like a fool and he or she might also think that the salesperson is trying to show off. This might even scare of the customer.

4.3.1 (c) Attitude

In simple terms attitude refers to what a person feels or believes about something. Additionally, attitude may be reflected in how an individual acts based on his or her beliefs. Once formed, attitudes can be very difficult to change. Thus, if a consumer has a negative attitude toward a particular issue it will take considerable effort to change what they believe to be true.

Organizations facing consumers who have a negative attitude toward their product must work to identify the key issues shaping a consumer's attitude then adjust marketing decisions, (e.g., advertising) in an effort to change the attitude. If the salesperson faces such kind of a customer he or she should also try to work to identify the key issues shaping a consumer's attitude then explain the benefits related to the product or service and steadily remove the negative attitude for the product, service or the organization.

For companies competing against strong rivals to whom loyal consumers exhibit a positive attitude, an important strategy is to work to see why consumers feel positive toward the competitor and then try to meet or beat the competitor on these issues. Alternatively, a company can try to locate customers who feel negatively toward the competitor and then increase an awareness among this group.

4.3.1 (d) Personality

An individual's personality relates to perceived personal characteristics that are consistently exhibited, especially when one acts in the presence of others. In most, but not all, cases the behaviours one project in a situation is similar to the behaviours a person exhibits in another situation. In this way personality is the sum of sensory experiences others get from experiencing a person, (i.e., how one talks, reacts). While one's personality is often interpreted by those we interact with, the person has their own vision of their personality, called self-concept, which may or may not be the same has how others view us.

It is important to know that consumers make purchase decisions to support their self-concept. Using research techniques to identify how customers view themselves may give marketers insight into products and promotion options that are not readily apparent. For example, when examining consumers a marketer may initially build marketing strategy around more obvious clues to consumption behaviour, such as consumer's demographic indicators, (e.g., age, occupation, income). However, in-depth research may yield information that shows consumers are purchasing products to fulfil self-concept objectives that have little to do with the demographic category they fall into, (e.g., senior citizen may be making purchases that make them feel younger). Appealing to the consumer's self-concept needs could expand the market to which the product is targeted.

4.3.1 (e) Lifestyle

Lifestyle plays a very important factor in the process of buying decision. For example there are two customers and both want to buy a mobile phone and the both have the same budget. But even though having things in common their lifestyles will determine the phones which they buy.

Infact lifestyle is the influencing factor which relates to the way we live through the activities we engage in and interests we express. In simple terms it is what we value out of life. Lifestyle is often determined by how we spend our time and money.

Products and services are purchased to support consumers' lifestyles. Marketers have worked hard researching how consumers in their target markets live their lives since this information is the key to developing products, suggesting promotional strategies and even determining how best to distribute products. The fact that lifestyle is so directly tied to marketing activity will be further examined as we discuss developing target market strategies.

4.3.1 (f) Motivation

Motivation relates to our desire to achieve a certain outcome. Many internal factors we have already discussed can affect a customer's desire to achieve a certain outcome but there are others. For instance, when it comes to making purchase decisions customers' motivation could be affected by such issues as financial position, (e.g., *Can I afford the purchase?*), time constraints, (e.g., *Do I need to make the purchase quickly?*), overall value, (e.g., *Am I getting my money's worth?*), and perceived risk, (e.g., *What happens if I make a bad decision?*).

Motivation is also closely tied to the concept of Involvement, which relates to how much effort the consumer will exert in making a decision. Highly motivated consumers will want to get mentally and physically involved in the purchase process. Not all products have a high percentage of highly involved customers, (e.g., milk) but marketers who market products and services that may lead to high level of consumer involvement should prepare options that will be attractive to this group. We would later in this chapter discuss motivation in detail.

4.3.2 External Influences

Consumer purchasing decisions are often affected by factors that are outside of their control but have direct or indirect impact on how we live and what we consume.

4.3.2 (a) Culture

Culture represents the behaviour, beliefs and, in many cases, the way we act learned by interacting or observing other members of society. In this way much of what we do is shared behaviour, passed along from one member of society to another. Yet culture is a broad concept that, while of interest to marketers, is not nearly as important as understanding what occurs within smaller groups or sub-cultures to which we may also belong. Sub-cultures also have shared values but this occurs within smaller groups. For instance, sub-cultures exist where groups share similar values in terms of ethnicity, religious beliefs, geographic location, special interests and many others.

As part of their efforts to convince customers to purchase their products, marketers often use cultural representations, especially in promotional appeals. The objective is to connect to consumers using cultural references that are easily understood and often embraced by the consumer. By doing so the marketer hopes the consumer feels more comfortable with or can relate better to the product since it corresponds with their cultural values. Also the salesperson should understand this and also respect the culture from where the customer is coming from. Additionally, smart marketers use strong research efforts in an attempt to identify differences in how sub-culture behaves. These efforts help pave the way for spotting trends within a sub-culture, which the marketer can capitalize on through new marketing tactics, (e.g., new products, new sales channels, added value, etc.).

4.3.2 (b) Other Group Membership

In addition to cultural influences, consumers belong to many other groups with which they share certain characteristics and which may influence purchase decisions. Often these groups contain opinion leaders or others who have major influence on what the customer purchases. Some of the basic groups we may belong to include:

- ***Social Class*** – represents the social standing one has within a society based on such factors as income level, education, occupation
- ***Family*** – one's family situation can have a strong effect on how purchase decisions are made

- ***Reference groups*** – most consumers simultaneously belong to many other groups with which they associate or, in some cases, feel the need to disassociate

Identifying and understanding the groups consumers belong to is a key strategy for organization and the salespeople. Doing so helps identify target markets, develop new products, and create appealing marketing promotions to which consumers can relate. Also design a pitch or an approach for the customer with which the customer is able to relate. In particular, marketers seek to locate group leaders and others to whom members of the group look for advice or direction. These opinion leaders, if well respected by the group, can be used to gain insight into group behaviour and if these opinion leaders accept promotional opportunities could act as effective spokespeople for the marketer's products.

4.3.2 (c) Purchase Situation

A purchase decision can be strongly affected by the sıtuation in which people find themselves. In general, a situation is the circumstances a person faces when making a purchase decision, such as the nature of theiı physical environment, their emotional state, or time constraints. Not all situations are controllable, in which case a consumer may not follow their normal process for making a purchase decision. For instance, if a person needs a product quickly and a store does not carry the brand they normally purchase, the customer may choose a competitor's product.

Marketers can take advantage of decisions made in uncontrollable situations in at least two ways. First, marketers can use promotional methods to reinforce a specific selection of products when the consumer is confronted with a particular situation. For example, automotive services can be purchased that promise to service vehicles if the user runs into problems anywhere and at anytime. Second, marketers can use marketing methods that attempt to convince consumers that a situation is less likely to occur if the marketer's product is used. This can also be seen with auto products, where marketers explain that using their product will prevent unexpected damage to their vehicles.

4.4 MOTIVATION FOR THE CUSTOMER

Different customers buy for different reasons. The salesperson has to understand what the customer needs and motives are. The salesperson should search for the underlying motives so that the salesperson can relate the selling points of the product or the service to the customer and help the customer to identify themselves with the product or service that is offered. Needs and motives are identified through questioning and talking to the customer. But the salesperson needs to always remember that each customer is different and he or she should design, plan and present themselves accordingly.

Abraham Maslow hierarchy of needs theory sets out to explain what motivated individuals in life to achieve. He set out his answer in a form of a hierarchy. All human need can be classified into five hierarchical categories and this hierarchy is universally applicable. These five categories are as under:

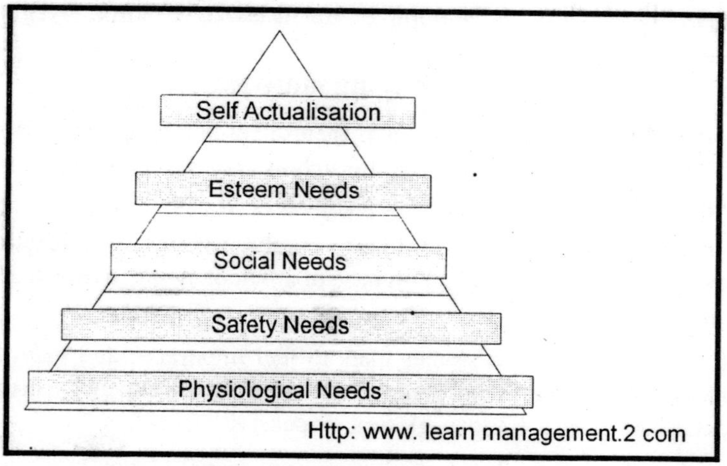

Diagram: Maslow's Hierarchy of Needs

- ***Physiological needs***: Food, shelter, sexual satisfaction, i.e, those needs needed for basic survival.
- ***Safety needs***: The need to feel safe within your environment. Also refers to emotional and physical safety.
- ***Social Needs:*** The need for love, friendship and belongingness
- ***Esteem needs***: The need for self-respect, status and recognition from others.
- ***Self-actualisation***: The point of reaching ones full potential. Are you capable at excelling yourself?

So, an individual will need to satisfy their most basic need before they can move onto the next. Only when that individual knows that they have met their physiological needs will they move onto their safety needs. Maslow suggests that if you wanted to motivate an individual you will need to know where within the hierarchy they are placed.

According to Maslow's hierarchy all needs can be ranked in order of importance from the low biological need to the higher level psychological needs.

Maslows concept suggests that needs change as we go along our path of striving for self-actualization. Supermarket firms develop value brands to meet the psychological needs of hunger and thirst. So Maslow's concept is useful for marketers as it can help them understand and develop consumer needs and wants. There are, however, problems with Maslow's theory. Firstly, it is difficult to tell at what level a person is at within their hierarchy and when that level has been satisfied. Also there is little statistical evidence to prove that this theory actually works. Never-less, it is popular and does have some weight behind it.

Some buying motives:
• *Comfort Need:* People like to give themselves pleasure and will respond to sales talk about the comfort of the upholstery, the smoothness of silk, the richness of colours of cushions, the texture of leather • *Recreation Need:* People may like to purchase things for relaxation. Play is a strong buying motive: e.g., Purchase of a indoor swing, a love seat, a rocking chair. • *Self Esteem Need:* A customer likes to feel important, and may desire high value, or branded items that signify high social status, expensive dressing table, Mont Blanc pen, a Rayban glasses, expensive cosmetics. • *Imitation Need:* E.g., The fashion conscious teenager may buy a product that is "in", or a woman might want a product worn by a film star or endorsed by a celebrity.

4.5 HOW CONSUMERS BUY

So now that we have discussed the factors motivating the consumer's decision to purchase, let's examine the process itself. This process is presented in a sequence of 5 steps as shown below.

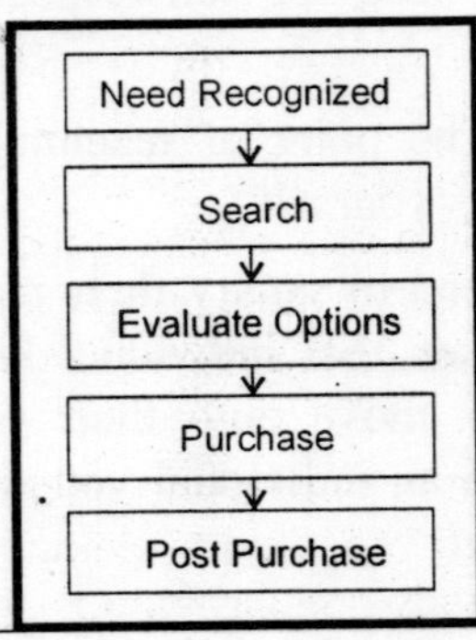

However, whether a consumer will actually carryout each step depends on the type of purchase decision that is faced. For instance, for minor re-purchases the consumer may be quite loyal to the same brand, thus, the decision is a routine one, (i.e., buy the same product) and little effort is involved in making a purchase decision. In cases of routine, brand loyal purchases consumers may skip several steps in the purchasing process, since they know exactly what they want allowing the consumers to move quickly through the steps. But for more complex decisions, such as major new purchases, the purchasing process can extend for days, weeks, months or longer. So, in presenting these steps marketers should realize that, depending on the circumstances surrounding the purchase, the importance of each step may vary.

Need/Want/Desire is Recognized

In the first step the consumers has determined that for some reason he/she is not satisfied, (i.e., consumer's perceived actual condition) and wants to improve his/her situation, (i.e., consumer's perceived desired condition). For instance, internal triggers, such as hunger or thirst, may tell the consumer that food or drink is needed. External factors can also trigger consumer's needs. Marketers are particularly good at this through advertising, in-store displays and even the intentional use of scent, (e.g., perfume counters). At this stage the decision-making process may stall if the consumer is not motivated to continue (see motivation above). However, if the consumer does have the internal drive to satisfy the need they will continue to the next step.

Search for Information

Assuming consumers are motivated to satisfy his or her need, they will next undertake a search for information on possible solutions. The sources used to acquire this information may be as simple as remembering information from past experience, (i.e., memory) or the consumer may expend considerable effort to locate information from outside sources, (e.g., internet search, talk with others, etc.). How much effort the consumer directs toward searching depends on such factors as: the importance of satisfying the need, familiarity with available solutions, and the amount of time available to search. To appeal to consumers who are at the search stage, marketers should make efforts to ensure consumers can locate information related to their product. For example, for marketers whose customers rely on the internet for information gathering, attaining high rankings in search engines has become a critical marketing objective.

Evaluate Options

Consumers' search efforts may result in a set of options from which a choice can be made. It should be noted that there may be two levels to this stage. At level one the consumer may create a set of possible solutions to their needs, (i.e., product types) while at level two the consumer may be evaluating particular products, (i.e., brands) within each solution. For example, a consumer who needs to replace a television has multiple solutions to choose from such as plasma, LCD and CRT televisions. Within each solution type will be multiple brands from which to choose. Marketers need to understand how consumers evaluate product options and why some products are included while others are not. Most importantly, marketers must determine which criteria consumers are using in their selection of possible options and how each criterion is evaluated. Returning to the television example, marketing tactics will be most effective when the marketer can tailor their efforts by knowing what benefits are most important to consumers when selecting options, (e.g., picture quality, brand name, screen size, etc.) and then determine the order of importance of each benefit.

Purchase

In many cases the solution chosen by the consumer is the same as the product whose evaluation is the highest. However, this may change when it is actually time to make the purchase. The "intended" purchase may be altered at the time of purchase for many reasons such as: the product is out-of-stock, a competitor offers an incentive at the point-of-purchase, (e.g., store salesperson mentions a competitor's offer), the customer lacks the necessary funds (e.g., credit card not working), or members of the consumer's reference group take a negative view of the purchase, (e.g., friend is critical of purchase). Marketers whose product is most desirable to the consumers must make sure that the transaction goes smoothly. For example, internet retailers have worked hard to prevent consumers from abandoning online purchase, (i.e., online shopping carts) by streamlining the checkout process. For marketers whose product is not the consumer's selected product, last chance marketing efforts may be worth-exploring, such as offering incentives to store personnel to "talk up" their product at the checkout line.

After-Purchase Evaluation

Once the consumer has made the purchase they are faced with an evaluation of the decision. If the product performs below the consumer's expectation then he/she will re-evaluate satisfaction with the decision, which at its extreme may result in the consumer returning the product while in less extreme situations the consumer will retain the purchased item but may take a negative view of the product. Such evaluations are more likely to occur in cases of expensive or highly important purchases. To help ease the concerns consumers have with their purchase evaluation, marketers need to be receptive and even encourage consumer contact. Customer service centres and follow-up market research are useful tools in helping to address purchasers' concerns.

4.6 SUMMARY

There are various types of purchases which a customer does depending upon the products/serviecs, for e.g., household food items vs clothes. One needs to understand that the product/service which you are selling is categorised under what kind of purchase for what kind of customer. Every purchase is influenced by various factors which could be either internal or external. Also every customer has some motive behind every purchase. This motive could be classified by Maslow's theory of motivational needs. After understanding the motives and then connecting it to the understanding of how customers buy, it becomes easy to identify. The customer needs the identification of customer needs act as a very important enabler in the whole selling proces. Thus, in simple words, if a salesperson or the organization is able to identify the customer needs it helps in boosting sales and increasing revenue and profits.

4.7 SELF ASSESSMENT QUESTIONS

1. Describe all the factors affected during one instance wherein you or your family member/friend has bought a certain product.
2. Write a note on "Internal influences or external inflences" which have a great effect on buying decisions.

5 IMPORTANCE OF PRODUCT

Chapter

Objectives

After going through this chapter, you will be able to understand:

- What is a product?
- Categories of consumer product
- Components of the product
- Key product decisions
- Features vs. Benefits
- Advantages of Branding and Brands
- Importance of packaging

Structure:

5.1 Product

5.2 What is a Product?

5.3 Key Product Decisions

5.4 Branding

5.5 Packaging

5.6 Summary

5.7 Self Assessment Questions

5.1 PRODUCT

Mr. Kapoor along with his wife and son visited a newly opened supermarket on a Sunday. He was very well greeted as well as his 4-year son was given a toy to play with so that Mr. and Mrs. Kapoor can shop without worrying about their son. Also, the staff's helpful nature was clearly visible during their regular offering of baskets whenever the premises was full and also helped them with the trolleys. The Kapoor's were very happy with the overall experience and had also decided to do their monthly shopping from the same supermarket.

But once they reached home they found some worms in the vegetables which they had bought. Due this the Kapoor's were very upset. All the good experiences which they had experienced had washed away. Infact Mrs. Kapoor said, "Our local vendor is good, he does not know how to greet the way these sophisticated supermarkets do. But at least he gives good vegetables."

Ultimately, the strongest buying motivation for the customer is the product or the service he or she is paying for.

Also many a times one will go to a store will have a lot of expectations. Jut to find out that their expectations are not met. One should remember in the store experience will motivate the customer to buy, but at the end when the customer is back home, the product or the services need to meet the expectations.

The most common problem that customers face is salespeople who have insufficient product knowledge. The result of this is that customers may find themselves having to make their own selection based on very little help or advice. When the customer comes to the store for a product or a service, it is the strongest motivation. With his product knowledge, the salesperson can swing the customer's mind, as most retail decisions are taken inside the store.

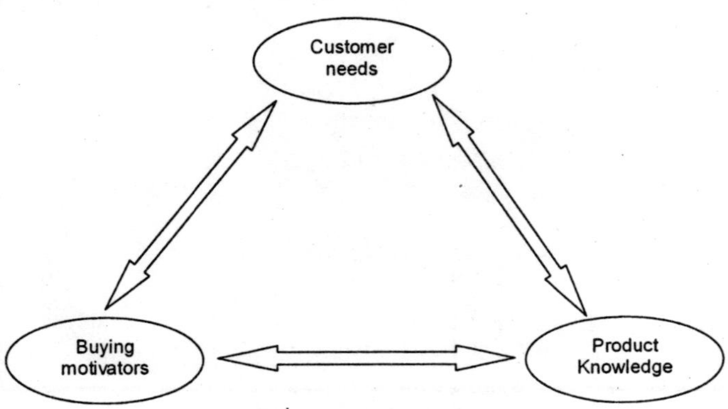

Three pillar model

All the three pillars form an important role in building and running a store or a business. Even if we remove one of these pillars or even if one of the pillar is weak, then the sales process may not be as effective as it should be, thus, resulting in lower sales.

5.2 WHAT IS A PRODUCT?

In marketing, the term "product" is often used as a catch–all word to identify solutions a marketer provides to its target market. We will follow this approach and permit the term "product" to cover offerings that fall into one of the following categories:

- ***Goods*** – Something is considered a good if it is a tangible item. That is, it is something that is felt, tasted, heard, smelled or seen. For example, bicycles, cellphones, and donuts are all examples of tangible goods. In some cases there is a fine line between items that affect the senses and whether these are considered tangible or intangible. We often see this with digital goods accessed via the internet, such as listening to music online or visiting an information website. In these cases there does not appear to be anything that is tangible or real since it is essentially computer code that is proving the solution. However, for our purposes, we distinguish these as goods since these products are built (albeit using computer code), are stored, (e.g., on a computer hard drive), and generally offer the same benefits each time, (e.g., quality of the download song is always the same).

- ***Services*** – Something is considered a service if it is an offering a customer obtains through the work or labour of someone else. Services can result in the creation of tangible goods, (e.g., a publisher of business magazines hires a freelance writer to write an article) but the main solution being purchased is the service. Unlike goods, services are not stored, they are only available at the time of use, (e.g., hair salon) and the consistency of the benefit offered can vary from one purchaser to another (e.g., not exactly the same hairstyling each time).
- ***Ideas*** – Something falls into the category of an idea if the marketer attempts to convince the customer to alter their behaviour or their perception in some way. Marketing ideas is often a solution put forth by non-profit groups or governments in order to get targeted groups to avoid or change certain behaviour. This is seen with public service announcements directed toward such activity as youth smoking, automobile safety, and illegal drug use.

While in some cases a marketer offers solutions that provide both tangible and intangible attributes, for most organizations their primary offering — the thing that is the main focus of the marketing effort — is concentrated in one area. So, while a manufacturer may offer intangible services or a service firm provides certain tangible equipment, these are often used as add-ons that augment the organization's main product.

Categories of Consumer Products

In addition to categorizing by type of offering, most products intended for consumer use can be further categorized by how frequently and where they are purchased.

- ***Convenience Products*** – These are products that appeal to a very large market segment. They are generally consumed regularly and purchased frequently. Examples include most household items such as food, cleaning products, and personal-care products. Because of the high purchase volume, pricing per item tends to be relatively low and consumers often see little value in shopping around since additional effort yields minimal savings. From the marketer's perspective the low price of convenience products means that profit per unit sold is very low. In order to make high profits marketers must sell in large volume. Consequently, marketers attempt to distribute these products in mass through as many retail outlets as possible.

- ***Shopping Products*** – These are products consumers purchase and consume on a less frequent schedule compared to convenience products. Consumers are willing to spend more time locating these products since they are relatively more expensive than convenience products and because these may possess additional psychological benefits for the purchaser, such as raising their perceived status level within their social group. Examples include many clothing products, personal services, electronic products, and household furnishings. Because consumers are purchasing less frequently and are willing to shop to locate these products, the target market is much smaller than that of convenience goods. Consequently, marketers often are more selective when choosing distribution outlets to sell their products.

- ***Speciality Products*** – These are products that tend to carry a high price tag relative to convenience and shopping products. Consumption may occur at about the same rate as shopping products but consumers are much more selective. In fact, in many cases consumers know in advance which product they prefer and will not shop to compare products. But they may shop at retailers that provide the best value. Examples include high-end luxury automobiles, expensive champagne, and celebrity hair-care experts. The target markets are generally very small and outlets selling the products are very limited to the point of being exclusive.

In addition to the three main categories above, products are classified in at least two additional ways:

- ***Emergency Products*** – These are products a customer seeks due to sudden events and for which pre-purchase planning is not considered. Often the decision is one of convenience, (e.g., whatever works to fix a problem) or personal fulfilment, (e.g., perceived to improve purchaser's image).
- ***Unsought Products*** – These are products whose purchase is unplanned by the consumer but occur as a result of marketer's actions. Such purchase decisions are made when the customer is exposed to promotional activity, such as a salesperson's persuasion or purchase incentives like special discounts offered to certain online shoppers. These promotional activities often lead customers to engage in impulse purchasing.

Components of a Product

On the surface it seems a product is simply a marketing offering, whether tangible or intangible, that someone wants to purchase and consume. In which case one might believe product decisions are focused exclusively on designing and building the consumable elements of goods, services or ideas. For instance, one might think the key product decision for a manufacturer of floor cleaners is to focus on creating a formula that cleans more effectively. In actuality, while decisions related to the consumable parts of the product are extremely important, the total product consists of more than what is consumed. The total product offering and the decisions facing the marketer can be broken down into three key parts:

1. Core Benefits
2. Actual Product
3. Augmented Product

1. Core Benefits

Consider what we have talked about many times in this tutorial; people make buying decisions that satisfy their needs. While many needs are addressed by the consumption of a product or service, some needs are not. For instance, customers may need to be perceived highly by other members of their group or need a product that is easy to use or need a risk-free purchase. In each of these cases, and many more, the core product itself is the benefit the customer receives from using the product. In some cases, these core benefits are offered by the product itself, (e.g., floor cleaner) while in other cases the benefit is offered by other aspects of the product, (e.g., the can containing the floor cleaner that makes it easier to spread the product). Consequently, at the very heart of all product decisions is determining the key or core benefits a product will provide. From this decision, the rest of the product offering can be developed.

2. Actual Product

The core benefits are offered through the components that makeup the actual product the customer purchases. For instance; when a consumer returns home from shopping at the grocery store and takes a purchased item out of her shopping bag, the actual product is the item she holds in her hand. Within the actual product is the consumable product, which can be viewed as the main good, service or idea the customer is buying. For instance, while toothpaste may come in a package that makes dispensing it easy, the consumable product is the paste that is placed on a toothbrush. But marketers must understand that while the consumable product is, in most cases, the most critical of all product decisions, the actual product includes many separate product decisions including product features, branding, packaging, labelling, and more. Full coverage of several of these important areas is provided later in this tutorial.

3. Augmented Product

Marketers often surround their actual products with goods and services that provide additional value to the customer's purchase. While these factors may not be key reasons leading customers to purchase (i.e., not core benefits), for some the inclusion of these items strengthens the purchase decision while for others failure to include these may cause the customer not to buy. Items considered part of the augmented product include:

- ***Guarantee*** – This provides a level of assurance that the product will perform up to expectations and if not the company marketing the product will support the customer's decision to replace, have it repaired or return for a refund.
- ***Warranty*** – This offers customers a level of protection that often extends past the guarantee period to cover repair or replacement of certain product components.
- ***Customer Service*** – This consists of additional services that support the customer's needs including offering training and assistance via telephone or online.
- ***Complementary Products*** – The value of some product purchases can be enhanced with add-on products, such as items that make the main product easier to use, (e.g., laptop carrybag), enhance styling, (e.g., cellphone along with Bluetooth earphones) or extend functionality, (e.g., portable keyboard for PDAs).
- ***Accessibility*** – How customers obtain the product can affect its perceived value depending on such considerations as how easy it is to obtain, (e.g., microwave stocked at nearby store, delivered directly to office), the speed at which it can be obtained, and the likelihood it will be available when needed.

5.3 KEY PRODUCT DECISIONS

The actual product is designed to provide the core benefits sought by the target market. The marketer offers these benefits through a combination of factors that makeup the actual product.

Below we discuss in detail three key factors that together help shape the actual product. These factors include:

- Consumable Product Features
- Branding
- Packaging

Consumable Product Features

Features are characteristics of a product that offer benefits to the customer. In most cases, the most important features are those associated with the consumable product since they are the main reason a customer makes a purchase.

The most important thing a salesperson needs to keep in mind is that a customer never buys features of the product it always the benefits that the customer buys. The benefits of consumable product features are classified into two groups: functional and psychological.

Functional Benefits

Are benefits derived from features that are part the consumable product? For instance, a plasma television includes such features and benefits as:

Feature	Functional Benefit
screen size	offers greater detail and allows for more distant
screen resolution	viewing provides clear, more realistic picture
surround sound	immerses all senses in the viewing experience
remote control	allows for greater comfort while viewing

Few more examples of features linked to benefits are as follows;

Feature	Link	Benefit
Real Teak wood table From the House of Durian	And this indicates Which means	Lasting for generations Full confidence that the piece has been quality tested
Contemporary oval shape and design	Indicates	Impeccable taste and makes a style statement in your dining room
Scratch-proof surface	Which means	The piece will look as good as new, even in 5 years,
Formal, long sleeved cotton salwar kameez	Means it is	Wearable to work and for evening wear
ABC company brand	And the benefit is	Full confidence that the shirt has been tested for durability
100% cotton	Means	You will be comfortable as it absorbs sweat
Fashionable style collar and colour options	Means you have	Wide range to choose from

These features are called functional because they result in a benefit the user directly associates with the consumable product. For marketers functional benefits are often the result of materials, designs and production decisions. How the product is built can lead to benefits such as effectiveness, durability, speed, ease-of-use, and cost savings to name just few.

Psychological Benefits

Are benefits the customer perceives to receive when using the product though these may be difficult to measure and may vary from customer to customer? These benefits address needs such as status within a group, risk reduction, sense of independence, and happiness. Such benefits are developed through promotional efforts that target customer's internal makeup.

In addition to determining the type of features to include in a product, the marketer faces several other decisions related to features:

- ***Quantity and Quality vs. Cost*** – For the marketers an important decision focuses on the quantity and quality of features to include in a product. In most cases the more features included or the higher the quality level for a particular feature, the more expensive the product is to produce and market.
- ***Is Better?*** – Even if added cost is not a major concern, the marketer must determine if more features help or hurt the target market's perception of the product. A product with too many features could be viewed as too difficult to use. This was often the case when video cassette recorders (VCR) were the principle device for taping television programmes and watching rented movies. Many of the higher-level features introduced in the 1990s as the product matured, such as advanced television recording, proved too difficult for the average consumer to master. To talk about the more recent example would be a mobile phone. Manufacturers try to fit all the possible applications into the phone. But many people (especially the old age) find it extremely complex to use the phone; some times they are not able to extract a phone number from the phonebook.
- ***Who Should Choose the Features?*** – Historically marketers determined what features to include in a product. For instance, companies offering website hosting services allow website owners to choose from a list of service options that best suits their needs. Also, for traditional products, such as clothing, companies allow customers to stylize their purchases with logos and other personalized options.

5.4 BRANDING

Branding involves decisions that establish an identity for a product with the goal of distinguishing it from competitors' offerings. In markets where competition is fierce and where customers may select from among many competitive products, creating an identity through branding is essential. It is particularly important in helping position the product in the minds of the product's target market.

While consumer products companies have long recognized the value of branding, it has only been within the last 10-15 years that organizations selling component products in the business-to-business market have begun to focus on brand building strategies. The most well known company to brand components is Intel with its now famous "Intel Inside" slogan. Intel's success has led many other B2B, companies and even non-profits to incorporate branding within their overall marketing strategy.

Brand Names and Brand Marks

At a very basic level branding is achieved through the use of unique brand names and brand marks. The brand names, which may be either the individual product's name or a name applied to a group or family of products, is important for many reasons including suggesting what the product is or does, (e.g., Big Bazaar, Mother care). The name is also what we utter when we discuss the product, (i.e., word-of-mouth marketing). The brand mark is a design element, such as a symbol, (e.g., Nike Swoosh), logo, (e.g., Yahoo! Graphic, Dell), a character, (e.g., MacDonalds) or even a sound, (e.g., AirTel tune, Reliance ADA group tune), that provides visual or auditory recognition for the product.

Advantages of Brands

A strong brand offers many advantages for marketers including:

- Brands provide multiple sensory stimuli to enhance customer recognition. For example, a brand can be visually recognizable from its packaging, logo, shape, etc. It can also be recognizable via sound, such as hearing the name on a radio advertisement or talking with someone who mentions the product.
- Customers who are frequent and enthusiastic purchasers of a particular brand are likely to become brand loyal. Cultivating brand loyalty among customers is the ultimate reward for successful marketers since these customers are far less likely to be enticed to switch to other brands compared to non-loyal customers.

- Well-developed and promoted brands make product positioning efforts more effective. The result is that upon exposure to a brand, (e.g., hearing it, seeing it) customers conjure up mental images or feelings of the benefits they receive from using that brand. The reverse is even better. When customers associate benefits with a particular brand, the brand may have attained a significant competitive advantage. In these situations the customer who recognizes he needs a solution to a problem, (e.g., needs to grab a quick bite) may automatically think of one brand that offers the solution to the problem, (e.g., MacDonalds). This "benefit = brand" association provides a significant advantage for the brand that the customer associates with the benefit sought.
- Firms that establish a successful brand can extend the brand by adding new products under the same "family" brand. Such branding may allow companies to introduce new products more easily since the brand is already recognized within the market.
- Strong brands can lead to financial advantages through the concept of brand equity in which the brand itself becomes valuable. Such gains can be realized through the outright sale of a brand or through licensing arrangements. For example, company A may have a well-recognized

Our private eye. Lugano

The end of the conventional advertising by Oliver like

Today large companiess have to invest the money that they used on conventional advertising campaigns into the product itself. Our theory, the CTP strategy (Communication through product) mentioned below, undelines the importane to improve the USP of a product through investing in its design and innovation. The product thereupon speaks for itself and hence has no need to be communicated through conventional ATL advertising as before.

The consumer of today's world is better informed than ever due mainly to the Internet. He is willing to pay a premium for a product but only if it communicates lifestyle to him. How can we acheive this? What are the rules to obey to get a positive result? would like to explain this to you through an example of the watch industry.

10 years ago I created a watch-brand called By picking one of the most en vogue designer at that time, Marc Newson, I differentiated the looks of the product from what was available in timepieces on the markets. Combining traditional Swiss mechanical watch making with avant-garde design was the key of my success. Design for me is form and function, it equals art and has function as well as, shows off an outstanding design, success is just around the corner.

The most important lesson I drew from the focus on the product design in the above example was that you have to be very precise in your briefing in order to develop a consistant brand strategy.

It should not be the designer who creates a product that he wans but is should be a team of market researchers from your company telling the designer what the market wants and then accordingly the designer will use his talent to interpret your briefing.

Through the different locks, its innovative mechanical functions and its coherent corporatc ıdentity Ikepod watches became known in the markets within a few months. We would never have been able to pay for all thé free editorials and PR that we received. The so called brand ambassadors (,ovie stars, pop stars, etc.,) bought the product at our retailers without us even being aware. We did not have to pay them anything for endorsing our product. I even recall to have received a phone call from Elton John's manager asking me to allow them to use our watches for the conventional ATL-TV advertising of the Royal Mall and they did buy watches for this Suddenly the Ilepod brand started to become a trendsetter. In the watch industry there a few big companies that also deived part or all of their success due to focussing on the procut design. What would Audemars Piguer be today without The Royal Oak watch-lines designed by Gerald genta. How would the sales

Ikepad watch by Marc Newson

have developed for Jaeger-le-Coultre without their Reverso model? How would Patek's image be without introducing the Nautilus or Aquanaut designed by the same Genta?

These are just a few examples that show you that if you le the product speak, through its design and innovation, you can save millions on conventional ATL advertising.

Here again are the main ingredients that I consider necessary to succed with a CTP strategy:

- Importance of an exact briefing: Firstly analyse your markets and find out who your main brand ambassdors are (clients, retailers, distributors?). Listen to thier needs before you even start creating a new product

- Choose at least two good industrial designers that know material properties as well as modern production technologies. This way you do not risk to be dependant on just one designer.

- Do not be afraid to spend money on the design to acheive as many USP's for your product as possible. You can recover this investment entirely through the premium price of your product.

- Develop a coherent brand corporate identity and a consistant product strategy. Spend money on creating or improving your CI (logo, graphics, catalogue, Internet site.)

You will in a short time see that the investment is much less than in conventional ATL advertising and the resultls will be more effective. By communicating through product you reinforce your brand and you create a lasting value. Some of your products may even write "design-history" and generations later people will still remember your brand because of them.

brand (Brand X) within a market but for some reason they are looking to concentrate their efforts in other markets. Company B is looking to enter the same market as Brand X. If circumstances are right company A could sell to company B the rights to use the Brand X name without selling any other part of the company. That is, company A simply sells the legal rights to the Brand X name but retains all other parts of Brand X, such as the production facilities and employees. In cases of well-developed brands such a transaction may carry a very large price tag. Thus, through strong branding efforts company A achieves a large financial gain by simply signing over the rights to the name. But why would company B seek to purchase a brand for such a high price tag? Because by buying the brand company B has already achieved an important marketing goal – building awareness within the target market. The fact the market is already be familiar with the brand allows the company B to concentrate on other marketing decisions.

5.4 PACKAGING

Let me ask you a question,

"Would you buy a plain looking item or something excitingly packaged that makes anyone drool?"

Packaging is a very important marketing strategy to glamorize your product in order to attract the consumer's attention. Sometimes packaging is so important that it cost more than the product itself in order to lure the consumers to buy it. Packaging should definitely be included in the 4 major Ps of marketing (product, place, promotion and price).

Most consumers judge a product by its packaging before buying. So it is logical to say attractive packaging is crucial in order to get the first time buyers to buy your products. Without attractive packaging, who would buy it in order to try it? Your first step to enter the market is crushed if the packaging is ugly.

Having attractive packaging doesn't mean you should neglect quality either. In fact, you need to make high quality products in order to have repeated sales. Converting first time buyers into loyal customers should be the main goal of your business and packaging is the door to it.

Packaging is the critical link between the product and all forms of promotion.

Packaging becomes more important as other promotional avenues are restricted or eliminated by law. Packaging displays are a highly prevalent and effective form of promotion. So-called "power walls" – large, attractive displays of tobacco packages behind the checkout at retail outlets – promote tobacco products at the critical moment when the consumer is prepared to buy.

Packaging conveys product characteristics even when the product itself does not. Product packaging strongly influences perceptions of the product.

Packaging and branding is not only important to young people, but also plays an important role in the buying decision across the age category. Especially products with a high degree of social visibility ask for an exclusive packaging. As users perceive their own personality in the brand image, and the brand image reflects back on them.

"The discrimination in product terms, pure build product terms, without any packaging or name around it is very limited... it's very difficult for people to discriminate, blind tested. Put it in a package and put a name on it, and then it has a lot of product characteristics."

Don Brown, than Vice President marketing, Imperial Tobacco, Canada (1989)

If you look at the packaging for the iPod, it satisfies the first point (product containment), and excels at the third (storage and shipment) because it is a cube. But what about the second (product information) and the fourth (branding)? What does the packaging communicate about the product? The answer is that the packaging simply and elegantly communicates that:

1. This is a premium product
2. This is a product from Apple
3. This is an iPod (assuming you know what one is)
4. Some product information (assuming you're pro-active enough to look at the bottom of the box)

Points to Remember:

After understanding the importance of the product along with the importance of the product along with the importance of pitching the benefits, it also important for the sales person to show that the product is valued and this can be exhibited by the ways in which the product is handled and physically presented to the customer.

For Examples:

(a) A necklace should be held gently between the forefinger and thumb rather than grasped in the full hand.

(b) A bottle of jam or squash or a exotic drink bottle is presented with one hand cradling the neck of the bottle while the other gently supports the base.

(c) A curtain or a bedsheet fabric is spread using both the hands.

The way product is handled by the salesperson or any other person in the store creates on value of that particular product in the minds of the customer. In fact some product knowledge is required by everyone working in the retail business, although the depth and range of knowledge will vary according to the role of the individual.

Few more points to remember

It is very important for a salesperson to know the complete details of the product. Following are few points that a salesperson should know about the products:

1. Complete and detailed product knowledge
2. What the product is, what it does and how it fulfils customer needs and expectation
3. Knowledge of range of products stocked, colours, sizes, prices
4. What the Brand stands for?
5. Schemes of both the store and the brand
6. Related products and accessories knowledg so that add-ons can be suggested

Few points on the importance of product knowledge:

1. The salesperson is the only person who can demonstrate to the customer, how a particular product fulfils his need.
2. The customer comes to the store for the product: it is the strongest motivator. With his product knowledge, the salesperson can swing the customers' mind, as most retail decisions are taken inside the store.
3. The salesperson is a product expert, a specialist, who knows everything on the product, and the only source of product information for the customer.

5.5 SUMMARY

However, good, the salesperson might be or even the ambience could be the best. But, if the product itself is not good, this creates a dissatisfaction in the customer which leads to loss of revenue. As a salesperson, one should have a thorough knowledge about the products and services which are offered not only by your organisation, but also the competitors. Major product decisions will also include branding and packaging as the key elements.

5.6 SELF ASSESSMENT QUESTIONS

1. Create a feature and benefit matrix for the following:
   (a) Mobile Phone with 3mp camera
   (b) Digital camera with extra zoom
   (c) Kurta with chikan embroidery
   (d) All weather shoes

(e) Ready to eat food packet

(f) Electronic massager

2. Write a short note on importance of product in the consumer buying decision.
3. Visit a recent Super/Hyermarket and list down the observed branding activities, their importance and impact.

6

Chapter

'BUYING' – A MEMORABLE EXPERIENCE

Objectives

After going through this chapter, you will be able to understand:

- How to involve the customer during a selling process.
- Importance and the concept of customer participation.
- Importance and the concept of customer reaction.
- Importance and the concept of buying signals.

Structure:

6.1 Customer Participation

6.2 Customer Reactions

6.3 Buying Signals

6.4 Summary

6.5 Self Assessment Questions

Today the information about any product is available at finger tips. Be it comparison for a highly sophisticated electronic gadget or may be simple wheat and rice. Infact one will find the retailers themselves distributing pamphlets, which provide all information of the product. Thus, those days have gone when the salesperson would hobble away at the customer in the hope that, eventually, some of his or her talks may wear down the customer, and the customer will give in and buy the product or service. Most customers today have very firm views of their own.

The best way to handle today's customers is by involving the customer. Thus, in this chapter we will be broadly discussing the following:

(a) Customer participation

(b) Customer's reaction

(c) Buying signals

6.1 CUSTOMER PARTICIPATION

Before even understanding customer participation and involvement, let us first understand the importance of this. As if once the salesperson understands the importance of involving the customer it will be very easy for the salesperson to adapt to the situation and involve the customer accordingly.

A customer while buying could think that – "should be look at other stores before purchasing."

"Do I really require this kind of product".

"Will I be able to use it to its full potential".

"Is it worth it?"

"Am I spending too much on this?"

"Will this colour really suits me or him/her for whom I am buying."

"Will this go along the colour of the well"

"Will it suit my personality?"

"I hope the after sales service is good".

"Should I stretch myself so much to buy this?

If the customer has any of the doubts in his / her mind it is essential to eliminate the same. As with the doubts in mind if the customer buys a particular product or service, and unfortunately if something goes wrong the customer will loose trust in the whole brand. Thus, the elimination of these doubts is of utmost importance, and the best way to do this is through customer participation and involvement.

Depending on which product or service the customer is looking at the involvement will also vary accordingly. It could vary from wanting to touch try out the product, asking for benefit statements or the after-sales service, also could be in the form of raising some objections about this product or service against others which they have seen, read or heard about such kind of elements of participation are quite natural and rather than to be seen as a nuisance, they should be encouraged as much as possible.

This could involve trying out a garment (trouser, shirt tops, kurta, skirt, etc.) thus, a visit to the changing or fitting room. In case of an electronic product this could involve asking for a demonstration, thus, able to judge the quality and the ease of usage. Each of these demonstration provides and excellent opportunity for the salesperson to encourage a positive comment from the customer like,

"These shoes suit your personality and I am sure they are soft at your feet as well, aren't they?

"Isn't it very simple to use? With only one press of a button, you get your washing a well as drying done."

"You can record your live match on the hard disk, Isn't that amazing?"

These kinds of statement encourage the customer to agree and this kind of agreement helps the overall impression that the buying decision is taken the customer, which is a well-informed decision. A customer should never feel he/she is been forcefully sold something, rather every customer would like to buy products or services themselves. Thus, it is the salesperson who needs to give this feeling to the customer by making the customer actively participate in the buying process (rather than selling process).

6.2 CUSTOMER REACTIONS

As a salesperson, one should be very careful in observing customer reactions on a continuous basis. Depending on the customer's reactions either positive or negative, the salesperson also has to handle the situation accordingly.

For successful sales, the salesperson needs to create a positive customer reaction. However, there are occasions when responses will not be positive, and this is when the special qualities of patience and determination will make all the difference to a sole.

The customer's reactions are very important and give the salesperson a clue as to what is going on in the customer's mind. Some customers give a positive reaction leading to a final deal. But there are other customers who give a negative reaction. These customers have to be dealt with a little care. In this condition, the salesperson has to be patient and has to try and motivate the customer. Let's see an example. There is this housewife who wants to buy a kitchen set for her home. One day she reads in one of the newspaper about some good offer on the kitchen set, and she then decides to visit the shop the very next day.

Customer "I have looking for a reasonably priced good looking kitchen set. Actually I read the offer you have placed on one of the kitchen sets in the newspaper yesterday".

Salesperson: "Yes, Mam, let me show you around."

Finally she has liked one of the kitchen sets.

Customer: "Is this the same set that you are giving discount on. "I think this is slightly different than the one that I have seen in your advertisement."

Salesperson: "Yes, this is slightly different. Its additional feature is that it differs in its style and colour contrasts which will give a different look to your kitchen. Also one of the most important feature of this set is that the material used in this set is highly durable and has better long lasting life as compared to others. Also, you can see its finishing has a different touch, isn't it? I am sure you have liked it."

A customer may have several reactions. But there are certain reactions which a customer always has like,

"What is the durability of the product?"

"If in any case I need to exchange the product will it be possible after I buy the product?"

This happens usually when a customer is buying apparels.

Let's see an example: There was a gentleman who wants to buy a shirt for himself. Finally he comes to the shop and has selected a few shirts.

Salesperson: "Sir, You seemed to have liked these three shirts, should I prepare the bill."

Customer: "Yes, but first I want to see the shirts fully opened out removed from the plastic packing. Because, it has often happened with me that when I see the shirts in the packing form, I like it, but when I go home and try them I don't seem to like them much."

Salesperson: "Fine Sir, I would open up the packing and show them to you so that then you can make up your mind."

Here, the salesperson has to be a little patient and tactful. He can bring up the positive points of the product during product presentation.

Customer Reactions Revisited

There are always various customer reactions but, it should be kept in mind that even if the customer's reactions are negative, the salesperson has to deal with them as a positive way. And, this then can probably lead to a sale because of change in the customer's thinking. It should be remembered that an negative reaction of the customer should never be retorted back in a negative or an arrogant way, otherwise it is for sure that the salesperson will never be able to make the sale.

Let's see an example: There is a customer who has visited a shop and is having a look at the imitation jewellery.

Customer: "Can you show me something that will go on my pink saree?"

Salesperson: "Sure, Mam here are some excellent jewellery designs in the colours of pink."

Customer: "Well, I feel these are either on the darker side or on the lighter shades of pink. I want actually a same pink as that of my saree. Do you have it?"

Salesperson: "Just a minute, let me just see if I have them". I think, this should be fine for you."

Customer: "No, but I haven't liked the design of this. It looks a little old fashioned and also it is costly and out of my budget."

Salesperson: "I think Mam, if you just try it on, you will feel the difference. These is a little difference in the shade, but I am sure it will go with your saree colour. It will give you an elegant and a sharp look. It is so elegant that I think you will not require to wear any other accessories to enhance your look, which will also prove cost-wise an economical purchase for you."

The salesperson should never be too pushy, otherwise the customer's objections increases and that results probably in lost of a sale. The salesperson has to learn to cleverly deal with the customer's objections. Rather than being very pushy, it is sometimes better to just leave it. Never retailiate in a negative way to the customer.

Instead at times you might just have to agree with what they say and do it in a friendly way rather than in a sarcastic way. Or then just to divert the customer's mind show them entirely different variety of products.

Let's see an example here: There was a young man who wanted to buy sports shoes for himself.

Customer: "Can I show some good sports shoes which would be comfortable for jogging."

Salesperson: "Yes, sir. Here, these are the good variety of sports shoes and will be comfortable for your feet."

Customer: "Yes, they are fine, but I find them a little too funky and expensive also."

Salesperson: "These sports shoes are in nowadays. And though they might seem funky to you, as they are actually but they are comfortable to wear. You can wear them on and then let me know your opinion."

Customer: "But, I think the colours are very bright and I don't like them."

The salesperson understood what the customer wanted to convey, so he didn't try to be much pushy.

All he did was, with a patient smile on his face, he put away those variety of shoes and told him, "Sir, Don't you worry. Let's forget these pair of shoes. I'll show you something that is new but according to your taste." So he brought in an another stock of shoes.

Salesperson, "I hope sir, you like them. These have just come in and also they are in light colours and probably in your budget.

Customer, "Yes, I think, these are the right type of shoes for me. I'll buy these pair of shoes, can you get the bill done?"

But then there are some customers who are actually not interested in buying. So, in these cases, the salesperson should leave the decision on the customer and not be much pushy. The salesperson should leave the deal in a decent and a clam way, so that if the customer wants to return again to his shop after visiting a few more shops, he should not feel hesitant to do so.

Buying Signals

Buying signals are communication signals that suggest the prospect is now ready to discuss how they can take ownership of your product and how it would specifically benefit and work for them. In other words, they are now proverbially sold on your product or service and are ready to discuss purchasing from you.

Buying signals: These are usually signals like questions and comments which indicate that customer is slowly getting committed to buy the product.

Buying signal has two types: Non-verbal signals and verbal buying signals.

Non-verbal signals: Here, again the salesperson plays an important role. He has to be observent and learn to observe the customer's body language like when a customer gets slowly interested in buying the product, he starts examining the product properly. For example, if it is a dress material, the customer will feel the material properly, will see in day-light, will put on her and have a look in mirror. If it is a shoe, the customer will see the flexibility, put on the shoes and walk a little and see if they are comfortable, see for the sole. These are non-verbal signals in which the customer is not in conversation with the salesperson but is on his own and is questioning and answering himself in his mind. And these signals have to be picked up by the salesperson.

Verbal Buying Signals:

These are actually the verbal signals, in which the customer converses with the salesperson and almost finals the deal. The questions asked or the conversations with the salesperson indicate that he is interested in buying the product. It is important that the salesperson does not miss these signals or sometimes it may even result in the loss of the sale. The verbal buying signals usually are like: Will you give me home delivery? How long do you take to deliver the product? Can I pay by credit card? If in any case, I want to exchange the product? Can someone come and demonstrate as to how to use the product?

These are few of the verbal buying signals that a salesperson must keep in mind which will help him to close the deal.

When customers come into your sights, they will be sending you signals.

The signals that they send will include:

- I am just wandering around with no real interest in products and intention to buy.
- I am interested in this product, but am not currently anxious to buy.

- I am very interested in this and might well buy it if you can answer a few questions.
- I want to buy this, now!

Buying signals usually take on the form of statements or questions from the prospect; these assertions or inquiries bring them one step closer to the comfort zone of making the purchase.

Buying signals may come in a variety of forms:
• A ***question*** might be a buying signal: "How soon can you deliver?"   • A ***comment*** might be a buying signal: "Sounds like what we've been looking for."   • A ***gesture, movement, or other non-verbal communication*** might be a buying signal: Suddenly you see a flash in the Prospect's eye, and he leans forward, picks up your sample and for the first time studies it closely.

If you fail to recognize the buying signs, you run the risk of overselling your product and missing the window of opportunity when a prospect is most receptive to becoming one of your clients. If you continue to share information or deliver your presentation to a prospect who has already communicated buying signals, that prospect can interpret this as in attention and or superfluity on your part. Either way, an inability to pickup on your prospect's signals may cost you the sale.

Buying signs can show up within the first few minutes of a conversation; or they may not emerge until the end of your meeting. In short, they can show up at anytime. It's up to you to hone in on these signals so that you can adjust your pitch accordingly and approach the close when it's most appropriate to do so.

Here is a list of questions that could suggest a prospect's interest to learn more or to buy:

- Are there any other styles or colours to choose from?
- How quickly can you get this (garment) altered?
- How much money do you need to begin this work/service? In other words how much advance do you need
- Do you offer financing?
- What type of warranty comes with this product?
- What type of service does your company offer?

- Are there any other types of warranty coverage available?
- How do take care of after-sales service?
- Are there any other discounts available?
- What sort of monthly instalment can you offer me?
- How will this work regarding my situation?
- What type of results could I expect?
- Are there any side effects?
- Will it suite my skin?

Questions on turnaround time, integration, installation, delivery, date or start of service, available features, expected results, product guarantees, and or instalment terms, colour choices, looking at fine print, all signal that you are closer to earning a sale.

Other questions that a prospect may ask can be drawn from past purchasing experiences. Those prospects who have had bad experiences in the past with either a company or a product will need to know that they are making the right purchasing decision with you. This can manifest itself as *support building questions* asked by the prospect.

Concerns over past problems indicate that a prospect may be a bit timid or sceptical. They are looking for the reassurance and support that they are making the right decision in using your services.

Here are some examples of a prospect utilizing support building questions:

- I purchased this computer one year ago. When I called the company for a service call, I found out they have already gone out of business. I certainly do not want to go through that again. What's your company's background?
- Last time I took a face wash manufactured by the same Brand, but had rashes all over my face?
- Is this for me?
- Are you sure that this is the best price you can give me?
- If I make this purchase, will this be the last time I will ever have to worry about this situation?
- Will this warranty cover all possible problems that may occur with your product?
- What doesn't this warranty cover?

- Can your competitors offer me something better?

You may find yourself in a situation where the prospect repeats the same question several times. Do not become annoyed. To repeat questions reveals the prospect's need for more assurance before he or she makes a purchase. The prospect may simply want to hear an answer more than once. It can also mean that they haven't fully grasped all of the information that you have laid out for them, and they need to hear it once more.

- Can you review what the warranty and service policy will cover one more time?
- Can you show me how your product works again?
- Will you go over those financing terms once more?
- So what this includes is ... ?
- And you are sure that once I start using this ... ?

When they are not ready to buy

When a customer is not ready to buy, it does not mean that they will not buy, but it does mean that you will need a different approach. Do remember also that if there are many customers around, spending a lot of effort selling to one customer may mean that you miss out on a lot of other easier sales.

Avoiding eye contact with you

When you look at them and they immediately look away, they probably do not need assistance right at this moment. Do watch what they are doing, because they may need some help soon.

If they are handling a limited range of products, spending time looking at things, then it may be a good idea to stand nearby, relaxed and ready to help (not anxious and ready to pounce). When they look at you with a longer glance, move toward them. If they keep looking, keep moving in and start the sale.

Making 'not now' excuses

If they say 'just looking' or otherwise indicate that they don't need help, then make an encouraging remark to keep them looking and back off. Still keep an eye on them to see if their demeanour changes.

Casual handling of the product

If they are casually picking up different products and dropping them back, perhaps not tidily, it can be a big nuisance for you as you tidy up after them (when they have left) but this may well be a symbol of a bored browser. As ever, keep an eye on them so you can move in when they change how they are behaving.

Looking at many different products

If they are wandering around looking at almost random products, spending a similar short time on each one, then they may again be a relatively bored browser.

Moving around quickly

When they are moving quite quickly around the place, they may be scanning for something or may be wandering. If they slowdown, watch more carefully and move in when they are showing more signs of interest.

When they are ready to buy

When the person is ready to buy, or at least they are showing some interest, then you should also be ready to pick them up and move them towards the final close.

Spending time looking at one product type

When they are looking at one type of product, and especially if you have a broad range from which they are browsing only a small category, then they may well be interested in buying. Perhaps they need advice, so ask if you can help them decide.

The longer a person looks at one product type, the more likely they are to buy it. They are investing their time, which is a sure sign of interest.

Looking around for somebody to help them

If you see them looking around, catch their gaze, and perhaps raise your eyebrows a little to signal that you are ready to help. If they sustain the glance or raise their eyebrows too, move in to sell.

This is particularly significant if they are holding the product or have just spend time looking at a limited product range.

Asking questions about the detail

If, when you offer help, they get into more details about the product, then they are likely to be becoming more interested.

If they ask about the functionality of the product, they may well have a checklist of things they are seeking, so ask for details of what they are seeking. You can also ask more about how they will use the product, from which you can advice on the best-buy for them.

Asking about price

This is a good buying signal. You can tell them the price or you can ask how much they are looking to spend today. If they tell you, then you can help them find the best value for the money they have to spend.

Using possession language

When they pickup the product, they are getting a sense of owning it. This continues when they talk about how they will use the product — which is a good reason for encourage this talk. Look for 'I' language. Get them to use it.

Ask how they will use it. You can even talk about it as if they already own it, although be careful of being unsubtle and pushy.

Asking another person's opinion

When they ask another person what they think about the product, they are likely thinking about buying the product and are seeking confirmation.

You might thus find yourself selling it to the second person also. Think about this when you are making the initial sale — include whoever else is there in the sales talking, though do watch for whether the main seller wants to be the main focus or appreciates others being included.

Body state changes

Any transition in non-verbal communication will typically signal a change in mental state that may well indicate readiness to buy. If they suddenly relax after asking questions or discussing the product, this may well signal that they have changed mental state. Other signals include changes in body position, gesture, skin tone, style of talk and so on.

Touching the money

If they touch their wallet or purse and especially if they get out cash or credit card, this is a very strong signal for you. Get to them and ask if you can help. If they say they want to buy, just take their money.

Points to Remember

Listen carefully to the customer's words

It's now the customer's time to deliver her carefully prepared and rehearsed purpose for the visit. Focus your attention on the customer's words. How clearly is the customer describing what needs to be done?

Take a look at the body language

Examine the customer's body position, gestures and overall demeanour. Do they support the customer's message? Is the customer asking you about your company's return policy in a gentle tone of voice with a smile on her face? Or is the customer asking about special delivery in a growling, demanding voice, while banging his fist on the counter?

Decide whether or not the body language supports the verbal message

If the body language is consistent with the nature of the verbal message, it is likely that the customer is saying exactly what he or she means to say. The body language appears to confirm the message. If the body language is inconsistent with the verbal message, it is likely that there is some ambiguity. In either case, you should not respond to the most likely message. Body language is subject to interpretation.

Determine the customer's most likely message

You only have an assumption of the customer's message, you have to find out whether or not your assumption is correct. Decide in your own mind what the customer is trying to say. If in doubt, follow the message from the body language.

Test your assumption, leading with the message from the body language

As we said earlier, body language is likely to be a better gauge of reality, but you can't be sure. So before acting on your assumption of the customer's body language, test for reality by asking the customer a question. For example, "I sense that you are not pleased with the service we've provided so far. How can we be of more help to you?" or "It seems that you like our store's return policy. Is this what you were looking for?"

6.5 SUMMARY

Every person wants to be treated good as well as wants to remember good instances. It is a salesperson we are able to make the buying process an excellent memorable experience for a customer, then not only will he/she give us repeat business, but also refer us to others. For doing so we need to make the customers participate in the selling process by looking at their reactions and understanding them appropriately.

6.6 SELF ASSESSMENT QUESTIONS

1. Describe the various buying signals displayed by the customer.
2. Explain in detail a good and a bad buying experience which you or any of your family member or friend may have come across.
3. List down the various aspects leading to memorable experience.

7

Chapter

CLOSING A SALE

Objectives

After going through this chapter, you will be able to understand:

- The importance of closing a sale
- Closing techniques

Structure:

7.1 Introduction

7.2 The Top Closing Techniques

7.3 Common Mistakes in Closing

7.3 Summary

7.4 Self Assessment Questions

7.1 INTRODUCTION

A truly good salesperson, whether they are selling consumer electronics, apparels or food, is a master at determining their client's needs and finding solutions for them. The sooner each salesperson realizes the importance of selling and closing and makes a decision to educate themselves on techniques and principals associated with selling and closing, the sooner the business will grow in turn improving their performance and sales.

Closing is the last step in the sales process; asking your prospective client for that final order or close the deal.

Although closing is a critical step, many people skip it unintentionally. They assume their prospect will automatically give them a sale. Although this does occur occasionally, closing the sale is as important as crossing the finish line at the end of a race.

Many people resist "closing" for fear of rejection. Don't be afraid to close and ask for the sale, whenever possible, at the end of the day that is reason why a salesperson is paid for. In the process closing, the salesperson is also facilitating the buyer in their buying decision. You will know when your prospects' interest is high, so take advantage of the timing by asking for their sale. Don't be afraid to close because in most cases, if you unsuccessfully attempt to close, you are both informing your prospect of your intent (to offer them your service/product) and you will receive an instant indicator as to where they are at in the sales process.

Frequently, people express interest by asking for details about you and your service. Use this as a guide that their interest is high and a close at this time could be the nudge that puts them over the hump. If they don't commit after your initial close, there is some type of objection standing in the way. Try to determine the objection or concern and, if you can address it, try to close again.

7.2 THE TOP CLOSING TECHNIQUES

Any sales is not complete until and unless it is closed. It is very important to understand that a retailer will get revenue only once the sale is done. Thus, closing a sale plays an very important in the overall business.

Do you think all customers come with the mindset of buying? So how can we tell who is serious and who is not? Some customers do change their minds in the process of buying, but some don't, so do we put a signboard saying "we will serve only those customers who are interested in buying our products. No, we can't do this. So the answer is we have to qualify the customer." Once we have qualified the customer correctly, there is no obvious reason why we should not have a real customer in front of us. But sometimes the customer is hesitating and has not yet expressed a serious commitment to buy. How can we obtain this? The simplest answer is to use the first closing method — ask or the order!

(1) Ask for it!

First of all the salesperson has to be very sure that the customer should not get any hint that a special "formula" is being used. The closing techniques should appear to be natural developments from the sales conversation. Let's see an example: There is this customer who wants to buy a shirt for himself.

Customer : "Can you show me some good shirts?"

Salesperson : "Would you prefer to see the shirts with a trendy touch or something sober for your formal wear?"

Customer : "I would prefer something sober and not so very bright colours."

Salesperson : "These are some of the best shirts that are according to your taste."

Customer : "I must admit, these are really very nice shirts".

Salesperson : "So, which would you like to buy, then?" "Is it the yellow or the white?"

Customer : "Just a minute, let me try them on first and then I will decide whether to buy or not".

On hearing this, perhaps the salesperson brought the rejection on himself. The salesperson had an optimistic feeling that the customer would buy without trying them on. But it didn't work. So the salesperson gave another try?

Salesperson : "It seems you are more inclined towards this shirt than the other shirts that you have tried on."

Customer : "Yes, it is very comfortable, but I still cannot make-up my mind. I'm just not too sure about the colour choices. Will the light blue or the light yellow one go best with my black trousers?" Could you help me? Which one would you recommend?"

Salesperson : "I think either of the colours would look fine on you and will go with your black trousers and give you an elegant look."

The customer is still confused and takes his time to make a decision.

Customer : "Finally, I think you are right. Both the shirts have a smart look."

Salesperson : "So have you decided then, which one to buy?"

Customer : "Yes, I will buy both the shirts. And thank you very much for being so patient. Actually it was going a little difficult for me to make the choice. But you have helped me out."

So, in this example we saw that the closing question grew naturally. Thus, an important learning from this example is that the closing question has to come out naturally out of the conversation. It has to be a natural resolution of the sales interview without the customer having any knowledge of this. The salesperson should therefore aim to avoid any "seams".

(2) The "Order Form" close

This method is different from the above mentioned method. This is a natural development from the technique described above. This method involves just a slight variation. The questions asked are not in direct reference to the purchase. This is the main difference. So the salesperson can rather put up a question saying "Sir, Do you want me to write up the order?" And this is the natural language which is usually used in your business. So, you would prefer to question in a slightly different manner saying, "Sir, shall I make out the invoice or bill?"

It is again important here for the salesperson to sound the natural and avoid any rejection.

Sometimes a direct question asked runs the risk of a rejection.

But sometimes you feel that this is the right time to try to close the sale, and still then you get an answer from the customer, "No, thank you". So then this would rather come as a surprise to you and you would wonder, "Why is that?" This would be a natural reaction. But it would be rather better for the salesperson to sound a little surprised. This help you gain some reaction from the customer which will further enable you to judge whether you are still "on target."

The salesperson can put forth to the customer saying, "Sir, I'm sorry, but I think I have misunderstood somewhere. I thought you felt that this was the best for you."

The customer may then reveal to you that what is wrong and why he or she is still undecided or in other words, is still not wishing to close the sale. This will help you in giving some knowledge regarding the customers thinking which can then be overcome.

(3) The alternative close

The alternative close method is usually seen in car salespeople. It is usually assumed by the car salesperson that a customer visiting the car showroom will definitely buy. The only thing that is not decided is the colour, style or shape. But it is assumed that customer "will buy". So when the customer visits the showroom, you might ask the question, "Which colour or style would you prefer?" So, if you think that the timing is correct and the customer is really interested in buying, he will reply with a positive approach. So the customer may reply, "I would like the blue Indica." This will give you an indication and assurance that the customer is committed to buy the product. So you may be rest assured that you are on the right track. But if your timing is not correct or if you are dealing with a "difficult or a "not so committed" customer you may get a reply saying "who said I would buy anything?" This will leave you with need to draw out the reasons for the rejection made. But this might seem a little difficult because of the way the rejection was made, so probably a skilled salesperson will avoid this method for he has the fear of rejection. So, the important part here is product presentation. It is the product presentation that will provocate the customer to do the final choice between the product options that were presented. So, it is hereby understood that the close is a natural follow-up of the product presentation.

(4) The summary close

This is the way used by the salesperson to say that "we have reached the end of the sale, so may just highlight the main points so that we could close the deal." This could be done by summarizing the list of benefits that the other person will receive, telling them the full extent of what they are getting for their money.

The summary close method is one of the most natural methods of closing. This method can also be used by the salespersons for those customers who are unpredictable. This is one of the most valuable methods which are used by the salespersons which proves to be beneficial. Here, in this method, the salesperson will have to summarise the sales interview so far done, and then finally ask the customer "So, sir, this is the one that you prefer, isn't it?" A customer who has finally made the decision of buying the product will reply, "Yes, this is the one that I like." So, this will presented as if it was a natural resolution during the presentation process. Thus, the summary close method is the most natural closing method. In this process, the customer should not recognize or even get a hint that the final question asked was used as a means of bringing the interview to a positive conclusion. But if the customer replies saying, "No, this is not what I want," the salesperson should re-qualify the customers needs.

Make it sound impressive, using full phrases and attractive words.

Go into detail, separating out as many sub-items and features as you can.

But also fit the description into a reasonable space of time. Your goal is to impress them with what they are getting, not to bore them with excessive detail.

Some examples are as given below:

"So as well as the basic product, you are getting free delivery."

"You could use the product and if you do not like it you could return it as you will be getting a five-day exchange assurance."

"This product or service is accompanied with our comprehensive guarantee."

"This comes in an easy-carry box and includes a remote control, with batteries included, of course!"

(5) The cautionary tale

The cautionary tale method is usually adopted to motivate the customer to decide in favour of the purchase of the product. This method often proves to be useful. Let's see an example:

Customer	:	"Suppose if I don't buying this dress today, do you have reasonable stocks so that when I come next week in town, I could come and buy it that time?"
Salesperson	:	"Well, I cannot give you an assurance, since this is a very busy time of the year for us. And at such times it becomes very difficult to obtain repeat orders. So, it might be quite likely that you might not get this dress, the next time you come." Only some ten days back one of the customers failed to close a deal on one of the dresses of a different style and said that she would come back in a day or two. But the next time when she came the dress was sold out to some one else, and then she Shad to make a choice of another dress of a different style."
Customer	:	"Is that so. In that case I feel I should buy the dress now that I have liked, otherwise I could be at a loss."

So, here in the above example an undecided customer was motivated to buy the dress of her choice.

But it is not that, the salesperson should cook up stories. It should just help the undecided customer to know the implications of failing to decide to purchase the product at the very moment. It is very important to keep the trust of the customer and hence the salesperson must not try to makeup false stories just to motivate the customers to buy.

But, sometimes it quite happens that the customer replies, "In that case, I don't have an option and probably I'll just have to take that chance." So with this the salesperson is left with no choice but then try another approach.

(6) The "Final" Objection

In this condition the customer sometimes has an objection right to the end of the sale but doesn't want to mention it probably because the customer feels either the objection point is very trivial to be mentioned of may be the salesperson may laugh it out.

For example: Let's say, the customer feel that the small embroidery work done on the dress doesn't go well with the whole look of the dress. And because of this she is in two minds before buying the dress. And at the very sametime, she feels that she cannot tell this to the salesperson as it is a very minor point. So, in this case the salesperson should try to unravel this objection and help the customer to come to a conclusion.

Salesperson : "Is it that something is bothering you regarding the dress pattern or colour, in any case? If it is so, you could let me know and I'll try to help you to sort out the problem."

Customer : "Yes, I am a little in two minds. I feel that the embroidery work done on the dress doesn't go that well with the whole look of the dress. Also I feel this will overall affect my looks.

Salesperson : "Yes, Mam, I think you are right. This dress will definitely affect your looks, but with a positive streak. It will give you an elegant and a new look." Also in another example, there was this young lady who had come to a shop to buy sunglasses for herself. But was a little too hesitant, as she was going to wear the sunglasses for the first time. Because of this it was going a little difficult for her to make the choice. The salesperson in this condition can help her out.

Salesperson : "What is it Mam, that is worrying you about the sunglasses? Is it the shape or the colour?"

Customer : "I am a little confused whether this pair of sunglasses will suit me?"

Salesperson : "It surely will Mam, as the dark colour of the sung lasses goes very well with your fair skin and the shape goes well with your face cut".

Customer : "Yes, I think you are right, I'll go for this then".

Thus, the point is that we need to know that there are some customers who are hesitant and have some last objection point which does not come out priorly. So, it is the job of the salesperson to try and persuade the customer to come out with the objection point if there is any, as this "last objection" affects their decision in the process of buying the product.

(7) The conditional close

This method can be used by the salesperson for those sorts of customers who are very slow in making decisions or are indecisive. These are the customers who actually want to buy the product but are usually finding an excuse or an "objection" just that they can delay their decision of buying the product a little later. The customer usually puts in a last question of worry saying that this is his/her main concern. At this point the salesperson should assure and confide the customer, that if any help is required they will be there at their service.

For Example: There is this customer who has come to buy a washing machine at a shop she was a little indecisive during the process of buying the machine, and has finally come up with the last objection.

Customer	:	"Are you sure that I will be available to wash my loads of bedspreads in this washing machine? Are you sure the dirt will be rinsed off properly?"
Salesperson	:	"Don't worry Mam, here is the brochure of the washing machine which has all the instructions written in it. And I assure you, that you will be able to find the answers to your questions in here."
Customer	:	"I think you are right, this brochure has answered all my queries. I feel a little satisfied and assured now, that I am buying the right washing machine. Thank you for being so helpful to me. It was kind of you."

In another example, there was this lady who had gone to a shop with her daughter to buy shoes for her.

After a long conversation with the salesperson she finally decided to buy the shoes for her daughter. But still she was a little unsure and then came up with a last objection.

Lady	:	"I just hope that these shoes do not hurt my daughter's feet, otherwise she will never wear them. And actually this is my main concern".
Salesperson	:	"Don't worry, Mam, these will definitely not cause any harm to your daughter's feet as these have been specially designed for children's feet. The leather of the shoes have been carefully selected and designed as per the needs of the children."
Lady	:	"Now, that was assuring that I have bought the best pair of shoes for my daughter."

So, the point here is the conditional close method can be very useful for the salesperson who feels that their customer is probably just looking for excuses for not buying. But the salesperson has to learn to put forth the conditional close in a subtle way.

(8) The "Lost" sales approach

The salesperson has to remember, that there are different types of customers and each one has to be dealt differently. Like some customers come with a definite decision to buy, see the products and purchase it. There are some customers who are very indecisive. And there are some customers who actually want to buy the product, have made up their minds, but at the end they have an objection. There are also some customers who are tense when they purchase something and lastly in the later stages of the sales interview they withdraw. And because of this the salesperson thinks that this withdrawal was caused personally due to him, which is not actually the fact.

So, in such situations the salesperson feels a little disappointed and loses all hopes. This is of course obvious to happen to the salesperson. But he should not lose hope and it is important for him to maintain a sense of balance. It is necessary for the salesperson to understand that there will be many times such occasions when he will lose a sale. But with further conversation with the customer it is quite possible that he might be able to do the deal.

Let's see an example: There was this housewife who was looking around in the shop for a reasonably priced dinner-set. But while looking around, she rather fell in love with the dinner-set that was costing slightly more than her budget. So now she was in two minds, whether to buy it or not.

Salesperson : "I think, Mam, this is the dinner-set that you were looking for. It seems you have liked it a lot".

Customer : "Yes, I have actually liked it, but I think I better not buy it this time".

Salesperson : "Don't worry, Mam, I think have a solution to your this problem. You are quite lucky in this matter as the company has specially provided a set of two plates and two bowls which are made of unbreakable material and that too with no extra cost. If you would give me an opportunity I would like to show the same".

Customer : "In that case, I would love to see it and reconsider my decision".

So, you see how a salesperson plays an important role here in helping and assuring the customer to overcome the "last objection"

(9) The trial close

A Trial Close is not a normal 'closing technique' but a test to determine whether the person is ready to close. The trial close works by putting the idea of closure into the person's mind. Their response will tell you whether they are ready or not.

Use it after a presentation or after you have made a strong selling point. Use it when you have answered objections.

The trial close may use other closing techniques or may be a more tentative question.

Ask 'If...' questions.

Ask questions that assume they have already bought the product.

When you have asked the trial close question, as with most other closes, be quiet, watching and listening carefully for their response.

Examples:

"It looks like you really like this. Is that true?"

"If you took it home, would you be proud to own this?"

"Do you prefer the larger or smaller version?"

"How would it look on the shelf back at home?"

The customer's response to a close must be followed-up appropriately. These closes are only a very few examples. There are literally entire books written on sales closes.

10. Assumptive close

Another effective closing technique is an "assumptive close". This is simply a statement that implies that you will do business with your prospect. Like the trial close, the assumptive close gets them to think of you as a service provider. It can also be used throughout the sales process to determine and build interest. In assumptive close the seller assumes that the prospective buyer has already bought the goods or services. Unlike the trial close, the assumptive close is usually posed as a statement, such as:

"We will deliver this hometheatre system by tomorrow evening."

"My engineer will install the system by tomorrow and by day after all the family members will be well versed with the system."

"When you do your next purchase we will give you a 20% discount considering your today's purchase."

The close should be a very conscious part of the sales process and when you enter into a closing opportunity, confirm that you have:

- Familiarized yourself with closing options
- Thought out ways to overcome objections
- Successfully created enough interest in your service
- Have mental and emotional clarity about closing
- Have clear pricing objectives
- Have prepared a way to accept payment
- Have an agreement or contract ready if necessary

7.3 COMMON MISTAKES IN CLOSING

Successful salespeople are often natural at sales and even more natural at closing. But closing a tough sale requires more than a winning personality. As any sales veteran will tell you, closing can be tricky, and there are many places where a false move can delay or derail a sale. You can boost your odds of completing the deal simply by avoiding these classic closing mistakes:

1. **Not asking for the business:** This we have also discussed earlier in the most important technique of closing. **"Not asking for the business"** is by far the most common mistake in sales. You would think it would be obvious: Either you ask for the business or you don't. But asking for business is more of an art than a science. Good, clear questions lead to successful closes but are often confused with requests for opinion and ambiguous queries, which do little more than lead to other questions. Rely on these classic closing techniques to help cut to the chase:
   - Summarize all the things the prospect said they want from a product or service. Use the notes you've collected throughout the sales process to show how buying from you satisfies these needs.
   - Highlight the extra benefits that your prospect will receive with your company's product or service.
   - Paint a positive emotional picture of how the prospect will feel when they use your product or service.
   - Show that the product is within the prospect's budget. If the price is a bit lower than expected, get them excited about it.

2. **Ignoring the prospect's signals:** Selling is more about listening than it is about talking. Your prospect may be ready to buy and you could be too busy talking to notice. After you've asked closing questions, stop talking. Let the prospect answer. It's tempting to keep selling when you should be listening, but you'll do a lot better if you learn to stop when you've said enough.
3. **Becoming jaded:** Attitude is everything in sales. Don't let past experience negatively affect your closing techniques. And don't let your successes cloud the circumstances of the current situation. Getting too caught up in the success or failure of each interaction can also be a problem. The best salespeople treat each new prospect as if they were the first and most exciting customer in town.
4. **Too Much Information:** Sales often fail to close if you gave too much information or too many choices. Don't show every model you carry or they may have to think it over. Too much information and too many choices set you up for a delay objection.

Points to Remember

ABC

ABC is a common term which stands for 'Always Be Closing', which is both good and bad advice.

ABC is good advice when it is used to keep in mind that you are always aiming towards a close. It is bad when you just use it to mean battering the customer to death with a barrage of unsubtle closing techniques.

Selling can be a lot like fly fishing. If you tug hard on the line, it will snap and the fish will get away. The best method is a gentle coaxing that gradually brings the fish in to shore — although sometimes when they are spooked you have to let them out again and calm them down further away.

Silence after

When you have used a closing technique, be quiet afterwards and let them respond. If you just keep talking, then you may miss what they have to say — like 'yes' for example.

Silence also builds tension and will encourage them to respond — and a response to a well-put closing question will hopefully be positive.

Watch emotions

Watch out for the other person not only in what they say but also in the emotions behind the words.

Never try closing when they are in a negative emotional state — you will only cause further objection and possibly anger that means they will never buy from you again.

Over-closing

It is not unknown for salespeople to talk their customers into closure then carry right on and talk them out again. You can over-do closing and it requires a close sensitivity to avoid this trap.

It is often the fear of the other person saying 'no' that often causes a salesperson to keep on talking. You must have faith and also accept that when they say 'no' it is no real comment about you. If you take rejection personally then you are probably in the wrong job.

7.4 SUMMARY

A sale is not complete until and unless a closing is done. Different situations may demad different kinds of closing. Also the clsoing technique may depend on the product or service a person is selling. Depending on that, he/she might decide to use any of the following.

1. As for it!
2. The "order Form" close
3. The alternative close
4. The summary close
5. The cautionary tale
6. The "Final" objection
7. The conditional close
8. The "Lost" sales approach
9. The Trail close
10. Assumptive close

7.5 SELF ASSESSMENT QUESTIONS

1. What do you understand by a 'Assumptive close' explain with an example.
2. Explain with an example, the difference between
   (a) Conditional close and Trail close
   (b) Alternative close and Conditional close

CASE STUDY

Structure:

1.1 Keeping Pace With The New Indian Consumer
1.2 Customers Are Forever
1.3 Relate To The Customer
1.4 Heed Complaints Diligently
1.5 Who's The Customer?

CASE STUDY 1

Keeping Pace With The New Indian Consumer

Rama Bijapurkar is an independent market strategy consultant and a recognised thought leader on consumer-related issues in India. A board member of some of India's leading companies — Infosys Technologies and Godrej Consumer Products, to name just two — she is also visiting professor at IIM-Ahmedabad, where she teaches marketing strategy. Readers of *Businessworld* will undoubtedly be familiar with her writings as she is a regular contributor to the magazine.

Taking stock of change in an environment where many changes are occurring simultaneously is daunting. One often searches for a way in which to capture all that has been going on, and figure out what it actually means for the way we think about things and the way we do things. That's why this collection of case studies is so useful. Starting from 1995 through to 2001, the cases document marketer's experiences, observations and assumptions about how their constituents have changed and the dilemmas they face on what they should, therefore, be doing. But even more insightful than the cases are the analyses. Every one of the case analysts has exactly the right background and experience to address the issues raised. And not one has disappointed or fallen short in bringing terrific clarity and perspective to the issues, and in proposing practical new frameworks to apply to the new emerging Indian market. That's why this selection makes for every enriching reading and reflection.

For this introduction, or '*sutradhar*' piece, as Meera Seth calls it, I have divided the cases into four broad into four sections: trade change, customer service, market strategy and human behaviour change. And all I am going to do is to what struck me as I read through them.

Trade Change

Clogging The Channels (Terrest India, Tea)

This case documents the toughening of the distributor, and his evolution from being a supplicant in a shortage economy to becoming the first point customer, aware of his to say 'no'. "No, I will not be dumped upon"; "No, I will not let you ride weak non-sellers on the back of strong sellers"; "No, I will not enable you to meet your unrealistic sales targets at the expense of my RoI (return on investment)." It also highlights marketing departments that are not performing their true role, busy as they are with their intellectual toys of TRPs (television rating points), packaging and advertising, and expecting the sales guys to deliver the numbers.

As case analyst Alec Lever (formerly at UniLever and now an independent consultant) says, "Did anyone in Til (marketing department) stand up and suggest (to the chairman) that attractive packaging alone is not relevant differentiation for a tea brand and so, why do a me-too, or in fact. a me-five launch of the new brand? "He also points out that the distributor is "no longer a man to grovel in gratitude to Til... for having chosen him over others... or even a 'partner in progress.... but is now Til's customer. who increasingly has a choice of suppliers to fuel his need for profitable capital growth". That's what competition does. And in this new world, as Alec Lever says. "market loyalty needs nourishment".

It is the specifics of this nourishment that Deepak Sethi of Mayar India lays out very clearly in his analysis. His new framework is thought provoking. because it demolishes traditional notions of sales being about push. And suggests the creation of a 'pull' culture in the sales and distribution organisation. Pull, as Sethi describes it, is assuring RoI to the distributor in exchange for services provided. And he spells out what this actually means in terms of changes in the sales function's role and job description.

Who's The Customer? (Kuello India, Skincare and Cosmetics)

This case shows another facet of increasing trade power — the arrival of the organised retailers, with many shops, adding up to sizeable turnover. Serving such retailers will require a new and very different orientation, and new skill-sets within sales organisations. Sunder Hemrajani, with his considerable experience in Whirlpool, Levers and Pepsi Co., suggests that a different sales organisation be created to focus on and cater to emerging segments. However, he cautions, don't take your eye off the ball on the traditional stocklist-driven system just yet, because the pace of consolidation and, hence, the rise of the organised retailer, should not be over estimated, since the *kirana* is still the lowest cost, highest customer service operator.

> Consumer markets appear more diverse today because there is an increased supply of brands, giving consumers a chance to express their individuality.

The mantra for the distributor-driven and the standalone multi-outlet retail systems is the same — delivering superior customer service. The mechanics of doing so are, however, very different, as is clearly described by the second case analyst who is a retailer — S. Murti of Food World. Murti presents the fascinating idea that organised retailers are actually a mega brand management team; marketers must gear up their sales and distribution outfits to support them in their role as brand builders. He describes the sales organisation required for providing such service.

Who Pays For Brand Building? (Neel Kamal Electronics)

This case lays out the idea that retailers need to invest in brand building for themselves to get customers to come. Both the analysts, Arvind Singhal of KSA Technopak and Rajiv Karwal of Electrolux, agree that in the case of durables, the retailer needs to differentiate himself from other retailers through the value-added services that he offers and encapsulate this in a brand that is communicated to consumers. Whether the cost of doing this has to be passed on to consumers, or whether it has to be absorbed by the retailer as an investment in his future has been debated. Probably not, says Arvind Singhal. Why not, asks Rajiv Karwal. If the customer wants the added services, he will pay. The larger message, though, is to the retailer. It is time to see yourself as a brand competing for the customer, and not just as a conduit for the supplier.

Customer Service

Incomplete solutions (Daffodils Computers); Customers Are Forever (Crysta Washing Machines)

Both these cases highlight the fact that compared to the past the weapon for winning market share is customer service and not product capability (now taken for granted and a 'must be' factor). "If I buy a computer, whose business is it to make sure that all the other stuff it needs in order to work smoothly is done?" (Theodore Levitt introduced the idea of the 'augmented product', which is the core product with all the services around it, way back in the 1950s. Judging from the Daffodils case, and our own experiences, I guess companies still haven't grasped it! Mukesh Aghi, CEO of Singapore-based Universitas 21 Global Pte Ltd, and Dinesh Puri, chairman of Altius Technologies, suggest that the problem of not being able to offer the augmented product is because multi-nationals in particular resist changing their behaviour for emerging markets.)

"Why is the servicing of my durables such a painful experience?" Sunder Hemrajani offers concrete suggestions on how to deal with complaints, while Dag Bennet, a UK-based academic, makes the important point that competition among marketers and, hence, the continuous improvement in offers to customers is what teaches customers to be more demanding and more sophisticated in their demands. I would tend to agree with that. Customers in the 1960s and 1970s were unhappy too, but complained less, or not at all, because they did not know what their rights were! Both analysts assert that the problem is one of managing the delivery of service and, presumably, though unsaid, managing the cost of good delivery.

Market Strategy

The Pricing Barrier (Tufflug Luggage)

This case captures all the shades of angst that we have been through all these years! The scene is so familiar. A dominant, well entrenched market leader, straddling premium, popular and discount price points, defining the rules of the market for customers and competitors. An underdeveloped market (read that as low penetration, infrequent purchase, category perception of utility and functionality rather than fashion or fun or any other value that people would be willing to pay more for). Mid and low price point; volumes are large, but grow slowly. High price point volumes are smaller, but fast growing.

Enter foreign brands. Of course, at the premium end. What will the consumer do? Jump at it? Or stick with the existing Indian option that has served him so well, so long, and over so many price points and product options?

The case analysis by Rajan Chhibba, previously at AF Ferguson and now at global strategy firm Intrim Business Associates, is very close to my heart. He points out that how, with smart product thinking, the consumer can actually be made to change. The new entrant can question who made the rules, and proceed to rewrite them in a customer relevant way. Change the way bags are stored — why can't they fit cupboards and lofts? Why can't people have luggage designs that allow you to carry wet towels and dirty laundry? Why are bags unisex when we know men and women carry different things? Why do we not have trade-ins to increase replacement frequency?

In essence, can 'shaper' actions by the marketer not change consumer behaviour, especially in categories where the huge dominant market leader has not bothered to do much? Isaac Jacob, the case analyst from the advertising business, also suggests shaper actions in the softer aspects of branding. Isn't there brand fatigue with the market leader, which can be exploited?

This case study was written in 1997, and now we have seen enough shaper actions which have made seemingly happy customers change behaviour in a jiffy. Two-wheelers are the best example of this. But then there has to be enough consumer insight to know when consumers are not ready to be shaped. Ask Kellogg's, Reebok, Coca-Cola or Seagrams.

> Kids have taken a quantum leap in awareness, discernment and decision-making. This means the marketer must self-regulate attempts to exploit them

A Fair Share For Everyone (Ambica Chemical Co.)

I think that this case study on the drawbacks of the takeover code is included in this section presumably to document customer orientation and change in regulator behaviour. Telecom regulation, though, is perhaps the best example of ever changing regulator behaviour, and it is the kind of change we would certainly like to see less of in the future!

Human Behaviour Change

The last four cases deal with how the Indian consumer is changing as a human being. They span issues of how children are different now because they are far better informed than the generation before them; their mothers are more educated and have stepped out beyond the boundaries of the home; and they have a different kind of relationship with their parents, who themselves are different from the generation before them.

These case studies also cover issues like the self-image and role models women of today subscribe to; people's attitudes to sex and how ready they are for bolder communication on taboo subjects; and how consumers spend their money in different ways nowadays, given that there are lots of exciting things other than FMCGs (fast moving consumer goods) now to spend on — and, therefore, how does a marketer of cooking oil fight to hold his own against mobile phones.

The analyses are insightful and provide perspectives on what is changing and what is not. There seems to be unanimity that women are confusing and come in many mindsets, and that "for every liberated girl there will be another willing and humble briden" (Anand Halve and Kiran Khalap, ad strategists).

The interesting point made in the case analyses on woman's magazines (Ashok Bhasin of Whirlpool and Sushil Pandit of The Hive in the case, 'Reading A Woman's Mind') is that consumer markets often appear to get more diverse, or segmented, only because an increase in the 'supply' of diversity (i.e., an increase in the number and diversity of brands) gives consumers a way to express their own individuality through brand choice.

There is also unanimity in the belief that kids have taken a quantum leap in awareness, discernment and decision-making ability, which demands a change in behaviour by the marketer to self-regulate attempts to exploit them as an economically influential adult group (media and marketing consultant Pratik Basu).

The key takeaway from these sections is that the consumer has indeed changed as a human being, but the trick, as Anand Halve points out, is "not to confuse apparent change (behaviour) with real change (beliefs)".

Kamini Banga of Dimensions Consultancy echoes this thought. In one of the *Businessworld* case analysis that appeared during this period (but is not included in this collection), she says: "[We must not] misread change in behaviour and attitude as a change in values and self-concept. It is values [notions of what is good and desirable], which actually shape attitudes and behaviour, and these can only change over long periods of time. *For example,* as a parent, one's attitudes may change from autocracy to dialogue, but basic values about bringing up children do not necessarily change."

CASE STUDY 2

Customers are Forever

Many companies forget their customer once the sales is done, without realising that customer services is a key differentiator in a competitive market

This case study was first published in BW, 7 May, 1998.

Tridip Roy walked up to his hostess, Kavita Khanna. "As a good friend, Kavita, you must now buy a Crysta washing machine," he said with a laugh. Roy had recently joined Crysta Industries as its vice president (customer services) and the dinner had been hosted in his honour.

Khanna's response was curt. "I do not want brand choices any more," she said. "A washing machine is a washing machine. From Videocon to Electrolux, they all just wash clothes. If there were differences in the quality of the wash, everyone would have upgraded their machines by now."

"What are you looking for in a washing machine that you haven't still found?" asked Roy.

"I want a company that knows how to handle a customer," she said. "So, don't tell me about computerised fuzzy logic or a noiseless drier. Tell me how different your customer service is. If your company uses an answering machine to record customer complaints, I am not your prospect."

That exchange set Roy thinking. In Khanna, he had seen a disillusioned customer complaints, albeit of a competing brand. But he could see that Khanna was not likely to repeat her brand purchase easily. He didn't want that to happen to Crysta.

For weeks now, Roy had been thinking about Crysta's future. As more and more new entrants stepped in, customer interest was declining. Every machine that its rivals sold meant a loss of opportunity for Crysta. But that was a smaller issue. The bigger problem was retaining Crysta's customers and market share. Roy firmly believed that Crysta's success as a brand lay in customer bonding. The company had to build relationships, along with the markets. Importantly, with Crysta planning to enter the areas of refrigerators and dishwashers, the market's faith in the brand depended on the image generated by the washing machine.

He told his managing director, Abhinay Talwar: "We already have a vast customer base. But when we launch our new products, will they choose our offerings over that of our rivals? Or, say, eight years from now when they want to replace their washing machine, will they again buy our brand? Today, we are concerned about the inroads the competition is making. Our efforts should be aimed at retaining our existing customers by building a strong bond with them."

Roy had seen that customers were getting more and more aware of product usage, whether it was a Crysta washing machine or anything else. "Let us examine the common grouses that customers have with the servicing and product delivery," he said to Girish Vyas, the customer service manager. "Customer service is an integral part of product delivery. It is an assurance of product performance from the manufacturer."

Roy had a unique plan. Since we want to ensure that our consumers stay with the brand, we need to find out why consumers change their brand, whatever the product. Let us meet 25 durable users, study their experiences with their current brands and find out if they are likely to buy the brand again", he said to Vyas. "Listen to every respondent carefully and tape her grievances, if necessary. Then we will tabulate them across common issues. The more we build into our service what they want, the more difficult will it be for our rivals to eat into Crysta's market share," he said.

Armed with the brief, Vyas set out to work. He met a wide spectrum of consumer durable users and listened to their experiences with their brands. Four weeks later, Roy heard the taped conversations of some of the respondents.

- **Archana Tull (owner of a water purifier:** Look at my water purifier. Last week, a person came to my house saying my service contract was up for renewal. Mind you, that was the first time in 10 months I was seeing anyone from Purifo. I did not like his barging into my time without prior notice. But that did not bother him. He had a list to clear, never mind if I was in the midst of cooking lunch.

I asked him about the servicing, since under the maintenance contract the company should have serviced the unit twice that year. "You should have called the company," he said. But that was a preventive maintenance contract and it was for the company to call and take a date.

Finally, he set about servicing the machine. I found that his handling of the machine was rather clumsy. He dropped the casing twice and strewed the carbon all over the sink. I discovered that he was just four months old in the company. Before that he used to sell plastic boxes. Is this what I get for being your customer?

Then he said the filter candle needed to be changed which I would have to pay for. That annoyed me. I showed him the contract which clearly stated that the company would replace the candle once a year at its cost. He did not know that. Would you believe that?

Clearly, such service contracts are simply a means to make money. There is no attitude to servicing. He came because it was February and had targets to complete in terms of contract renewals. He came without calling, expecting that we would drop everything else to serve him. He had no clue what he had to give the customer for the contract. He messed up my kitchen and did not even attempt to tidy it up.

The worst was that when I started the machine, the water would not flow. I was furious. I tore up the contract and told the guy to leave. Purifo sends incompetent, inexperienced people because it wants to cut costs. I carry the responsibility of providing my family a safe, hygienic environment at home, so I am prepared to pay for preventive maintenance. But what did I get?

But it is a good product and I am an informed consumer who knows how to work around a manufacturer's inefficiency. I simply gave the service contract to a private firm. I don't want to have anything to do with Purifo.

Ritikant Sharma (credit cardholder): Every month, I receive a credit card bill and my payment is sent the very next day. Five months ago, the bill did not come on the 22nd as it normally would reach me by the evening. I received the bill 10 days later with a charge of Rs. 675 for overdue interest. I was taken aback and called up the bank again. But the bank manager argued that the bill had been sent earlier. It was my word against his.

I wrote to Monet Bank, protesting against this undue charge. Eventually, after six letters from me, including one to the managing director, the bank "waived" the interest. But I was left with a bitter taste in the mouth. I wondered why the bank did this to me. Did I deliberately delay payment? I had this card for three years and not once had I defaulted on payment.

I also wondered if the bank considered the cost of this argument with me. Was it worth the Rs. 675? Why was the customer not right this time? And what about all those times when I paid four days before the due date? I was amazed by the way the bank treated me like an errant schoolboy. Since then I have not felt good about using the Monet credit card.

Worse, every month the bill continues to show the overdue interest and every month there is a fresh exchange of letters on the matter. Only last week I received an invitation to become a member of another credit card company. I am planning to surrender the Monet card.

- **Divya Mathur (owner of a washing machine):** You say I am an important customer of Crysta. Great. But for your customer service cell, I am just a number. For six months now, I have been having problems with the washing machine. Last month, when I called to follow up on an old complaint about the motor, the lady who took the call asked me to repeat the details again: model number, date of purchase, etc. When I pointed out that all these details had been given several times before and all she needed to do was check the complaint order number, her response was shocking, "May be, but I can't boot the system. I am only standing in for someone who has not reported today, so you have to give the details again," she said.

Tell me, what am I getting for being your customer? Respect? Good handling? No. Now you come here and ask me personal details like family income, number of members, and husband's designation at his job. You still haven't told me why you need all this information. You are researching. Are you collecting this information to help me or your company?

Then there was the problem with the V-belt. Within a day of replacing it, there were some creaking sounds. The engineer said he would have to wait for the senior supervisor to examine it. Reason? "We recently changed our supplier and all his pieces are turning out to be defective." I was taken aback. It frightened me to know that there was no quality check at your end. We outsource a lot of stuff for our garment business, but every button and needle is checked before it is used. We are not a multi-national, just an old family managed business.

- **Radhika Iyer (school teacher):** That feeling for the customer is simply not there. The customer is not a person but a collective noun. If the customer was important, wouldn't my water purifier company tell me when it changed the service agent? When I called the number in my contract card, I discovered that the number now belonged to a courier company. I had to call the head office in Mumbai and get the new service agent's number in Delhi.

Is this fair? Or does it matter? I guess the company's attitude was, "if a customer needs service, let her break her back and spend money to find out who the new agent is". The only motives are profits and sales volumes. Not customer loyalty and service. Therefore, a customer is one why buys your product, not only who has bought your product. Once you have bought the product you are a 'has been'. Why would you, or anybody else, want to invest energy in a set of people to whom a sale has been made? You spend energy as long as a sale is not made. Once a sale is done, it is for the customer to invest energy in sustaining his relationship with the manufacturer. Isn't that how it is?

The manufacturer's attitude is — you need me more than I need you, so guess who should work harder?

And every once in a while, there is a new face at my door asking me if I own a Zento purifier. Dammit, don't you have a customer file to give you that answer? No, he says. We go from door to door. Splendid. Then what do you do with all the data you collect? And every one of these men asks me the same questions: when did you buy it, what is your model number, is it working properly? The worst is: "What is your address?" I don't care what the information is being used for. But I don't want to be disturbed for information which you already have.

We believe that because India now manufactures Coke and Mercedes, we have progressed. But this new market is no different from the grey market, where you can buy anything but cannot expect service. For instance, I bought a packet of macaroni which said I had to boil it in 250 ml of water. I did that, but after the prescribed five minutes of boiling, there was enough water left in the pan. I then boiled it for another three minutes, and the pastal dissolved into a unrecognisable mass.

One day, I met someone who worked for this macaroni company. I told him about my experience. He said I should let the pan rest for five minutes after turning off the heat and the residual water would get absorbed. That worked. Couldn't the company have said so on the pack? Or is it cheaper to let the consumer invest in learning? Does the company use experienced hands-on cooks while designing these products or are they MBAs who can't tell all stove from a cigarette lighter?

I bought a jar of mayonnaise the other day. The label said it should be used within six months. Of what? Of the date of manufacture or the date of opening the seal? Do I refrigerate it or not? It takes us back to what I said before; once the sale has been made, the consumer does not matter anymore. The sale was not on the customer's involvement, loyalty or satisfaction. It never was and it will never be.

- **Dipankar Baruah (pager owner):** There are numerous messages that are flashed on the pager to announce the sale of wedding suits, printers, shoes, or TV programmes, or updates on cricket scores. These messages usually send out a single short beep. Only personal messages are announced with a long continuous beep. Last week, I was distracted by six ad messages for a chocolate. And all of them were long beeps. It made me mad because I was in the midst of meetings with clients and that kind of triviality is distracting.

The pager is a great device. It helps me catch messages which I would otherwise have missed. But I don't want it to distract me during a meeting. Please respect my privacy. The pager is for my convenience, not for the convenience of callous advertisers. Now, I leave the pager with the secretary and she calls me only if the message is a personal one.

Tell me, has the advertiser benefited? He sought to get his messages across to 1,50,000 subscribers at one go. It appears to me that my pager has become a cheap medium for advertising. Since it has done me the favour of selling me the pager, the pager operator can pass on my personal details to advertisers without even asking me. The pager is a private medium of communication, not a public address system like a radio.

We have allowed a million new products to enter the country, but along with that we have not allowed the market mindset to I evolve or grow. So, few people realise that the customer needs to be treated with respect.

- **Beryl Dias (owner of a laser printer):** This printer cost me Rs. 28,000. It was not funded by my company. I saved for it for a year. Let me tell you, saving that kind of money was not easy. I wanted the best, which is what I thought I got when I bought it. It worked very well and I know it is a good product. But that is where my ecstasy ends.

One day, the paper jammed and I needed help. So I called up the company. The lady who took the call said: "You will have to bring the printer here, we are not going to come there." That was very hostile, I felt. However, I expressed surprise that their service engineers would not come to my home. The lady gave me a silly reason: "If your mixie breaks down wouldn't you take it to the service centre?" Maybe she took the liberty to talk down to me because I was a woman and because I operated at home office. But there's a word of a difference between a Rs. 2,500 mixie and a Rs. 28,000 printer. But she was surely from the word go. Worse, their office was located very far from where I lived and going there would mean wasting my entire morning.

But her surely behaviour angered me the most. I recall how the sales engineers hovered around me when I had first contacted the company for a brochure. For three weeks, someone from the company would call me practically daily. They virtually pushed me into buying the printer. I remember I still had the last Rs. 1,500 to save up, when they decided to give me a Rs. 1,000 discount to hasten my decision. I was mesmerised by their sales pitch. Today, I am just a statistic. I can almost hear them saying: "You have no choice. If your printer is not working, that's your problem. If you live afar, that's also your problem!"

I had not considered the after-sales trauma when I bought the, printer. Like other products, I assumed that the company would come home to repair it. They did not tell me about their service terms at the time of the sale. It was not important, I guess. For all they wanted was my Rs. 28,000.

To repair the printer, I went through an agent who lost my complaint order papers, forgot to intimate the company about the part I wanted and made me wait for four weeks before the printer was repaired. And then I discovered that it hadn't been repaired at all. That's when I decided that I wouldn't have anything to do with the company ever again. I sold that printer and bought another brand after ascertaining that there was a service agent closeby. My old printer may have been state-of-the-art, but the real differentiator is the effort a firm is willing to put into customer service.

- **Vaidehi Chari (owner of a dishwasher):** I was looking for a dishwasher and visited several dealers. Although an advertisement had announced a festival discount on a particular brand, it was not available anywhere. Then I found one dealer who had a display piece. But he knew nothing about the machine. He had no clue about its capacity, its water consumption, or even its ability to work under low water pressure. He did not even have the product brochure. Even as I asked him questions, he simply walked away to attend to another customer.

Eventually, I bought another brand, for three reasons. One, it was affordable; two, it was a desktop model; and three, because it washed dishes. But the sale was made not by the salesman, but a friend who was a satisfied user. Strangely, she had warned me that the sales staff knew nothing about the product.

The demo was sketchy — I was left to learn a lot on my own about stacking the dishes, about rinsing, about pre-wash, about different brands of detergent. The detergent pack simply said: 'Follow manufacturer's instructions'. The manufacturer did not have enough copies of the instruction manual. I feel that manufacturers today know only how to make a sale. They don't know how to handle their customer after that.

- **Shalome Vaz (owner of a music system):** I have a poor view of the new entrants, which is why I refuse to buy any of these new music systems. My brother bought one of these complicated CD players from a high-flying Japanese firm. A year later, one of the speakers developed a fault. When he took it to the service agent, the engineer charged him Rs. 900 for the service. He kept the system for four weeks and returned it saying it was back in order.

Three months later, the same speaker failed again. This time, the engineer said a particular part had to be replaced and that would cost us Rs. 4,000. When you pay Rs. 16,000 for a CD player, you had better be ready to pay for expensive parts. But when the bill came, the engineer had again charged Rs. 900 as service charge. That was when we got mad. The last time, he had simply made do with the old part because he did not have stocks of the spare part. How were we responsible? Why did we have to pay Rs. 900 again? The service company stood its ground. As for us, we wanted our Rs. 16,000 player back so we grudgingly paid the Rs. 900. But you can see how we were being taken for a ride. I guess these foreign players see Indians as ignorant, gullible and desperate for their products.

Roy was amazed. He had heard many such complaints at social gatherings and from family members. At that time, they had a different flavour. Now, in the context of his research, he saw these people as customers, prospective users. Brand loyalty was not merely a function of product satisfaction, he realised.

> Roy relised that for Crysta to retain its customers and expand its market share, the company had to invest in customer service. That, he believed, was the most important investment for the next sale.

The products these people were talking about were mostly the new offerings of a liberalised economy. In a span of only five years, a great number of new products had inundated the market. But, as some respondents rightly assessed, the manufacturers had only focussed on the sale, moving from one sale to another, leaving the customer holding the product. They had done little to offer after-sales care. Not after sales-service, but after sales care. That was critical in forging a lasting relationship with the consumer.

Even among products that were not new to the Indian market, like refrigerators, he could see the rush to grab only volumes. Specifically, none of the innovations introduced in the newer models was being translated into real benefits by fitting it into the customer's needs. He recalled the time when he bought a four-door refrigerator. His wife had asked the service engineer how the bigger, deep freezer compartment could be put to use. The engineer simply told her to buy a cookbook that gave details of freezing. "It is ideally suited for freezing large amounts of meat, so you don't have to go out to buy it every time you need it," he had added as an afterthought.

For the vegetarian Roys, the fridge suddenly seemed a waste. His wife felt she could freeze vegetarian food also but the service engineer had no idea how that was done. "You will learn as you go along", he said. That was what she did. She spoke to friends and discovered that she would have to invest in deep freezer boxes and ziplock bags.

Roy had wondered why the manufacturer had not added value by producing booklets on freezing or offering a set of freezer boxes as a promotional offer. That would have helped the brand gain real value in the minds of users, he felt.

That was what bothered him very much at Crysta too. Merely manufacturing a product to meet basic needs hardly required foreign technology, he felt. If these were really global brands, why were they not taking pains to address the real needs of the consumers?

So, soaps, shampoos, washing machines and refrigerators were being offered in an underdeveloped market without consulting the consumer. "We just assumed two things", Roy said to Vyas. "That the propensity to consume and purchasing power existed here. Everyone thought there is hunger, so feed it. But how many of these products actually fitted into the needs of the consumer? Specifically, did any of these companies consider life after a sale?"

Roy was going to change a lot at Crysta. He wrote to Talwar: "A sale is not complete when the receipt for the cheque is issued. A sale is never complete. It remains alive for the life of the machine and the buyer. The customer is forever. That cost is the most critical investment for the next sale. Can we strengthen our mission to read, 'Our customer is forever, we will forge and sustain a relationship, like our relationship with our employees'?"

CASE STUDY 3

Analysis I: Dag Bennet

Relate to the Customer

Dag Bennet is deputy director, Center for Research in Marketing, London South Bank University. He's also as visiting professor at CEU Luis Vives in Madrid and the University of South Australia.

PEOPLE don't stop buying from a company because they find another company with a better product. They stop buying because they feel their company doesn't love them anymore. Tridip Roy is discovering how companies and customers relate to each other.

It may be stretching it a bit to talk about the customer company/relationship as one based on love, but the customer comments in the research are full of emotion, feeling and longing for something more. Most of the comments are also quite personal and not just because the company representative was human, but because people find it very difficult to have a relationship with a 'company' or an inanimate object. This is one of the reasons companies spend so much time and effort on developing brand 'personalities'. It's what people can relate to.

The research subjects here are peeved at a company or its representative — which they rightly perceive as one and the same. The comments are negative because these people feel they have been let down. And while they have an 'I can top that flavour', they illustrate the problems firms face in a world of increasing product parity — customer sophistication and expectations are rising when competitive activity is increasing. Witness the comment, "a washing machine is a washing machine". They may be wrong to some degree, but it is the perception that is critical; to this person, all washing machines are the same. Any supplier that talks to her about product attributes misses the point because she has gone beyond the product to consider other issues such as how she feels about the company and the quality of her relationship with it. She feels she is being taken for granted and this makes her angry.

- **Conditioning, Savviness and Sophistication.** Consumers rapidly become conditioned to competitive activity such as advertising, promotional activity and trial offers. With experience, they also become sophisticated evaluators of products; they expect what they buy to do what it is supposed to. In a competitive world, if products don't satisfy them, customers switch.

> People don't stop buying from a company because they find a better product. They stop buying when they feel ignored by the company.

Sophistication manifests itself in several ways. For example, there is usually a big difference between first and second-time buyers of office equipment in the attributes they rate highly. First-time buyers usually place price at the top of their considerations. Second-time buyers usually place price in the top five or so, but they rate other attributes such as reliability, performance and service higher.

> Service is vitally dependent upon people, and people cannot be viwed as inter-changeable cogs in the corporate machinery.

Rational firms try to ensure their products are at least as good as their competitors'. And they also try to come up with improvements that give some sort of advantage, however fleeting. Customers expect all products, from CDs to shampoo, to evolve. Furthermore, with competitors always trying to do something new, the customer can ask: "What have you done for me lately?" Failure to convincingly answer the question means not only that the customer feels let down in the relationship, it probably also means a lost sale.

- **Customer's Contract Point.** It seems and the main problem with customer service in this case is that the various companies cited have placed poorly motivated, inconsiderate or even untrained staff in direct contact with customers. The impression they convey is that they don't know what they are doing. It is easy to see how dangerous it is for a company which may receive thousands of phone calls each day. A mishandled phone call here and there isn't so important. But for the individual customer, a mishandled complaint or service call is 100% of their current contact with the company. Clearly, each call is much more important to the client than to the firm.
- **Not A Matter Of Good Luck.** Good customer service is designed into company operations and reflects corporate philosophy. Only now are managers waking up to the fact that service is vitally dependent upon *people* and that people cannot be viewed as inter-changeable cogs in the corporate machinery. At least, not if they are going to effectively handle the client-company relationship. In this case, the unhappy stories come from sophisticated, experienced customers who have to deal with unfeeling, unthinking cogs.

Customer service, therefore, must begin at the philosophical level, recognising that anyone at the point of contact with: customers must be trained in all aspects of the product or service, must be empowered to take decisions to resolve problems and, above all, must view customer service as critical to the success of the firm. This requires management attention, time and resources.

Tridip Roy is beginning to get the first inklings of the problem ahead of him. He may be beginning to see that 'relationship fatigue' is really just the most obvious sign that customer service is not integral to the firm's operations. Which is another way of saying that the two parties have grown tired of each other? Or, they don't love each other anymore.

CASE STUDY 4

Analysis II: Sunder Hemrajani

Heed Complaints Diligently

Sunder Hemrajani is executive director (sales), South Asia Business Unit, PepsiCo India Holdings.

Liberalization of the Indian economy brought about a dramatic change in the market. A number of new players, including multi-nationals, entered the country, thereby giving customers a choice like never before. From a sellers' market it became a buyers' paradise where the final verdict on the brand is the customer's. Kavita Khanna delivered her verdict when she said: "I do not want brand choices any more."

The proliferation of brands and models has indeed confused the customer. To customers like Khanna, tangible features like fuzzy logic or a noiseless drier, which played an important role in the sellers' market of yore, cannot be the key differentiator. It is indeed an intangible factor like customer service which is going to determine brand choice.

This is a lesson Roy learns at the beginning of his stint as vice president (customer service) at Crysta Industries. Roy realises that in the business of white goods, where competition is present, retaining customers is of utmost importance since the cost of gaining a new customer or regaining a lost one is going to be prohibitive.

The impending entry of Crysta into the refrigerators and dishwashers business presents Roy with an opportunity to leverage the brand equity built through customer satisfaction on washing machines in pushing new product categories. In an era of changing lifestyles and exchange offers, a reduced purchase cycle should enable the company to sell to the same customer if it could satisfy the customer about several issues during the life of the appliance.

Roy's attempt to study users of consumer durables is meant to understand the drivers of customer satisfaction which lead to brand loyalty and enable Crysta to get a customer for life. The feedback Roy gets from the respondents is quite clear. It highlights all the underlying factors that contribute to customer satisfaction. Unsatisfactory purchase experiences and sketchy demonstrations created a wareiness in Vaidehi Chair's mind when she wanted a dishwasher. It is well - known that in white goods, the decision-making process culminates in the shop and effective demonstrations lead to a favourable purchase decision.

For that matter, delayed delivery and installation can lead to dissatisfaction and loss of sale and goodwill. Divya Mathur's experience with a Crysta washing machine and Radhika Iyer's with macaroni left them highly dissatisfied with the product they had bought. Brands are expected to deliver what they promise. Any erosion in performance delivery can be a source of irritation in establishing long-term relationships.

Archana Tuli, Beryl Dias and Shalome Vaz are victims of poor after-sales service. Tuli's experience with the water purifying machine highlights the role of human resources in establishing customer relationships. Apart from the failure of the after-sales service process, it underscores the need for training in products, services and handling of customer complaints. Service contracts cannot be used only as revenue enhancement tools. Customer complaints offer opportunities to regain customer trust and to identify areas for improvement. In a competitive world, grievance handling is an opportunity to earn loyalty and a tool for brand building. Fewer complaints and lower satisfaction can be a silent killer. Organisations like Crysta would need to:

- Handle complaints in a manner that regains customer trust as fully as possible. The company's response should be prompt, fair and courteous.
- Use a systematic process to receive, document and analyse formal and informal complaints, identify underlying causes and translate the findings into corrective or preventive actions.
- Measure complaint resolution through appropriate indices, such as percentage of complaints resolved on first contact, response time and actions taken. The results should be tracked and used to derive improvement.

A requisite for building a lasting relationship is 'customer care', which is the way in which a company deals with a customer after a product purchase. It goes beyond product quality and fulfilling the basic needs. Monet Bank lost Ritikant Sharma as a result of not caring. Customer care can be enhanced through education programmes, product brochures, and simply by being polite and courteous. The product care booklets ensure involvement with the brand and lead to repeat purchases. The 'care' philosophy also addresses issues like respect and trust in the customer relationship. The pager and the printer companies violated these norms.

Customer satisfaction is the trust measure of a company's quality. Excellence in customer satisfaction is the key driver and measure of success. It is the foundation on which profitable businesses are built and sustained. This requires knowing customers and their expectations thoroughly. Knowing customers, in turn, allows companies to establish standards and requirements to manage relationships effectively.

A customer is best satisfied when she least expects it. Most organisations stagnate around very basic customer satisfaction levels — that is, meeting basic customer expectation is considered adequate. Successful companies enhance satisfaction by moving beyond customer expectations — by anticipating needs and surpassing them with superior products and by introducing surprises into the service programme.

Had the printer company given Beryl Dias a service call through a mobile service van within hours, or given her a service printer if the defective one had to be taken away, Beryl would have been delighted. A free service call outside warranty, or an unexpected zero-interest finance option at the point of sale can send satisfaction soaring.

As the customer is singled out for delight, the ripple effect will spread to many new potential customers. Companies should be prepared to delight the customer again and again, thereby increasing satisfaction at each encounter with the customer. Yet, delight today is expectation tomorrow. Therefore, Roy would need to continuously listen to customers' expectations and delight them. Crysta can be successful only if customers select its products over its competitors. Giving them reasons to do so will be a priority. In fact, maintaining customer focus will be the common thread woven through the company's strategic architecture. A score in excess of 90% on satisfaction drivers will be an ambitious, but not an impossible target. With that, Crysta will retain customers like Kavita Khanna for life.

CASE STUDY 5

Who's The Customer?

There was growing realisation at Kuello that its customer was not so much the end-user and the retailer, who was responsible for the success or failure of its products.

This case study was first published in BW, 7 December, 1998.

Rajan Misra was fascinated by the website supermarket. Scrolling through the site, he read the procedure for using the services it offered and scanned the products and brands that were available. He noted that barely two or three of Kuello Industries' skincare and cosmetic brands were listed.

Misra was vice president (sales) at Kuello Industries and took a lot of pride and care in ensuring the shelf presence of his skincare and cosmetic ranges. Although website supermarkets were still in their infancy in India, he noted the absence of his products on the list. That bothered him. He called Sudhir Gupta, the sales manager for the western region, and said: "Find out more about this website market and the person who runs it, and place all our brands on it."

Gupta was wary. "I have never heard of this man or his supermarket. Do we really want to get involved with these things?" he asked.

"I won't dismiss him so summarily, at least not in today's times," Said Misra.

"How many people buy on the web, Rajan?" asked Gupta. "Fifty, hundred?"

"It's not the numbers. This website retailer heralds the shape of things to come. Don't treat him lightly. I'd say, get to him before your competitors do," said Misra.

Gupta thought about it. Kuello's sales system allowed the company to sell only to its stockists. "The stockists are our customers and it is for them to sell to retailers," said Gupta. "I will ask one of our stockists to contact the website market."

Misra perked up. "Who is our customer?" he asked.

"Anyone who buys our products," said Gupta. "That is just one part of the definition," said Misra. "But first, let us examine who a consumer is. The 'consumer' is defined as the person who is the end-user. He does not necessarily have to be the purchaser. A customer need not be the consumer. An important part of being a customer is the existence of a purchase or sale. He may buy a product to give it to another for his or her use, like a mother who buys a soap for her child. Or he may buy goods to distribute them to a market of consumers, the way a stockist does."

"True. Therefore, the woman of the house and a stockist are both customers," said Gupta.

"But there is a difference," pointed out Misra. "According to the first part of the definition of a customer, a stockist can be a customer, because he purchases. And, for us, he is the first point of sale. Traditionally, therefore, we have looked at him as being the customer, because he purchases. And, for us, he is the first point of sale. Traditionally, therefore, we have looked at him as being the customer until we realised that there is the second important part of a customer in definitional terms — which is, that a customer must have a choice."

Gupta was unsure. "What are you trying to say?" he asked.

"Okay, tell me, does the stockist have a choice of what he buys?" asked Misra. "What is the motive behind his purchase decision? He buys because he has an agreement with us. Once he has undertaken to sell our products, he cannot buy from our competitor. His undertaking is for a fixed period and for only our products. He has no choice. He is a conduit to the end-consumer who has a choice. But because the stockist has no choice, he is not our customer," said Misra.

Gupta was surprised. "Then what is he?" he asked.

"He is our partner," said Misra. "The very fact that there is a contractual relationship affects our perception of our relationship with him, because we then start looking at issues like how we can manage his business better, how we can give him a good rate of return, how we train his people, so that they can, in turn, deliver our products to the market. He is an agent. He is merely a stopover in the distribution route. When you look at it from that viewpoint, the customer in our business is the retailer, because he has a choice which he can exercise. If he doesn't want to stock our brand, he will not buy it."

The retailer was more important because, unlike the stockist, he could influence what a company supplied to him. He was the conduit to the consumer

Misra now pushed the sheet of paper he was writing on towards Gupta. It read: 'A customer is a person who buys a product, who has a choice that he can exercise and a choice that can be influenced.' "It assumes the coexistence of two factors," said Misra. "One is your power to influence his choice and, two, his power to exercise that choice."

As Misra explained, while advertising allowed Kuello to influence the end-user's choice, in the case of a stockist there was no such power, simply because he was already wedded to his choice of brands by contract. Likewise, said Misra, the stockist could influence what a company supplied to him, but only to a limited extent. And that was decided by the customer, the retailer, for the retailer decided what he wanted to buy.

"Therefore, shouldn't the focus of our sales, distribution and marketing effort be the retailer?" he asked. "After all, he is the guy who has the choice and, if you do not influence him well enough, he will buy from the competitor. Therefore, this totally reorients how we look at our business. Now look at your website retailer and decide if he is important to us or not," he said.

Gupta got the drift of the discussion. "What does this reorientation have to do with the end-user?" he asked.

"Very simple," said Misra. "The retailer is the point at which an end-user seeks the satisfaction of his or her needs. And this is where we should structure our businesses. In the case of our skincare products, a consumer seeks to address her entire needs. So she wants a soap, a cream, a lotion, a lipstick, an eye shadow, a sun screen... what happens if her retailer cannot supply her with the entire range of products? She will either buy only a part of her needs or not buy from him at all."

"You are assuming that when a consumer goes to buy, she would like to see the entire range of products," said Gupta.

But Misra was going one step further. "Ideally, she would not like to go to two or three shops to meet her needs. But if she normally shops at the local store, where she gets her basic soap and cream, she cannot meet her entire skincare needs. For instance, if this retailer does not stock Gloderm, our anti-wrinkle cream, her need may be met by another brand."

"Therefore, we need to first target the retailer," continued Misra. "Because if we don't service our customer, the retailer, properly, somebody else will take him away from us."

Misra explained the dynamics of the retail pull and the end-user pull. Earlier, loyalty was dependent on gradually building a relationship with a brand. "Today the end-user is getting information on wrinkle management from everybody who is in the skincare business," he said. "Each is telling her about balances and hydroxy acids. She doesn't need to depend on what Pond's or Avon is suggesting. Given the knowledge base, she tends to become indifferent to brands. Her loyalty is to a category than to a brand. She may have a certain liking for Kuello's Gloderm, but Gloderm is not available at Royal Stores. So what does she do? Royal stocks Avon, and that delivers the same performance as Gloderm. So she could end up buying Avon."

"At the sametime," explained Misra, "look at it from the retailer's viewpoint. He asks his stockist for Gloderm, but, say, the supply is erratic. He could very well buy a substitute brand, because he is not bound to Kuello or any company with an agreement. And whose decision is he influencing? The end-users."

"But he has already made that decision for her by stocking Avon," said Gupta.

"And what has Kuello done?" asked Misra. "It has lost the slot on the shelf to Avon. But we are not talking about shelf-space. We are talking about the retailer's preference list. Why has he chosen Avon and not Gloderm? Because your service to his outlet is not good enough; you are not well represented in his shop."

Misra felt that a consumer who sought skincare was looking at a vast range of skin aids simultaneously. Hence, Kuello — which made lotions, moisturisers, sunscreen lotions, soaps, face scrubs, etc. — should ideally present its entire range as a portfolio to her, under one unified window, where all products come under one category or business group. "Therefore, shouldn't a company categorise its businesses according to what a consumer wants?" he asked.

Kuello manufactured three broad categories of skincare products — soaps, skincare products and coloured cosmetics. These categories were managed as three distinct profit centres. "As far as I can see, all these products must come under one umbrella for marketing and distribution," Misra said. "The consumer is looking at a menu that will meet all her skincare needs. This starts from the basic level of washing the skin to moisturising it, dewrinkling it, night repairing it or sun screening it till the cosmetic stage of dressing it up, painting it and preserving it. That is the need you are addressing, and that need cannot be fragmented."

Likewise, from the retailers' perspective too, he saw how Kuello could organise its businesses. "If a consumer wants a total solution, a unified window, the customer — that is, the retailer should be able to give it to her. Right?" he asked.

Misra put forth more reasons for shifting the focus to the retailer. Important among these was the growth of supermarket chains in some parts of the country. "In Chennai or Bangalore, you have FoodWorld and Nilgiris. In Delhi, you have

Nanz. These supermarkets have something like 20 outlets each. Now this supermarket retailer is very different from other retailers. Earlier, a retailer meant one outlet. Now, when the Nanz agent comes to me, he is talking about 20 outlets, he is a big customer."

More than selling the product, the retailers were selling a shopping experience. In the case of the virtual reality shop, the consumer sought that experience online.

This man was reaching out to more people, and he had the power to influence the buying habits and brand preferences of a larger segment of consumers. As Misra said: "If he says he does not want Gloderm, he does not want it for all 20 outlets." That meant Kuello would lose out on the opportunity to be present in 20 large outlets which were self-service stores, where significant numbers of end-users went to buy their entire week's requirements — from meat, eggs and flour, to soaps and cosmetics.

If a consumer went there to buy her entire skincare needs, it was because this supermarket was more likely to have a wider range of such products. Therefore, if Kuello was present there with all its products, there was a greater probability of her selecting Kuello's brands rather than those of others. It, therefore, seemed appropriate to Misra that Kuello should now be promoting its entire skincare mission under one umbrella.

"As a company, are we really doing that, addressing a consumer's needs in totality, as a total skincare solution?" I asked Misra. "Second, are you recognising that the people who are actually stocking your products can now influence or impact your off takes so much? Earlier you were looking at a retailer as one outlet or two outlets, but today this guy is offering a variety of brands tastefully stocked in each of his 20 outlets all over Chennai."

The large supermarket style of shopping was catching on among the urban consumers. Some of these outlets were trying outlets innovative ways of attracting the consumers, like offering shop credit cards against which a consumer could buy her entire month's needs. "This means that in places like these, the number of visits to the store is reduced. And when the consumer does visit these stores, she makes her brand decisions for the entire month. For example, she will buy three jars of Milo that will last the entire month, or two jars of Gloderm. Can you see what a great brand driver such stores can be?" asked Misra.

"Therefore, in the face of this retail revolution, shouldn't we reorient the way we are distributing our product?" he said.

Last week, he had a taste of this imminent revolution. Sitting in her Churchgate office, his wife had faxed her month's requirement of provisions on a computerised 'standard list' provided by her *kirana* store on Pali Hill in Bandra, which promised to deliver it at no extra cost. "And do you know, starting January 1999, he will accept e-mail orders?" said Misra incredulously. "This means more people will buy from him and more consistently."

Kwality stores was all of 400 sq.ft., had four delivery boys and sold over Rs. 20 lakh worth of goods every month. "Kwality Stores is important for us," said Misra. More than servicing, his priority was to persuade the store to stock Kuello's brands rather than the competitor. Of the six face washes in the market, Kwality stocked three. However, it did not stock Gloderm face wash. "Now think about it, 800 households who shop at Kwality will be cut off from Gloderm. See? It's not the numbers, it's the opportunity," said Misra.

This really meant that while Kuello targeted the end-user in its advertising, it could be leveraged only with some additional inputs to the retailer, who had now become very relevant. "What use is it then if our stockist carries Gloderm, when the retailer doesn't buy it? If the stockist is a mere stocking and distribution point he has very little bearing on the purchase decision of the retailer. The retailer is more critical and a very different creature in today's times. I feel that the field is not geared to or capable of handling this new avatar. Today's retailer is armed with computers that give him accurate details of how much stock was bought, when and by whom, and what his stock keeping units (SKUs) were. He has bar-coded his stock and knows the minute details of his purchase pattern and what it is doing for his sales," said Misra.

Like most other companies, Kuello too focused on stockists. Its field force dealt with the stockists whose sales force, in turn, dealt with the retailer. Misra now dropped a bombshell. "We should do away with the stockist sales force's interaction with the retailer. They should at best be order takers, not influencers, because they neither have the brand commitment nor the drive to influence the retailer. In other words, our field force should deal with the retailer directly."

Misra proposed that they begin by implementing this idea with the supermarkets. "If you superimpose the Kwality phenomenon on Nanz or FoodWorld, the ramifications are huge. Twenty stores, large volumes, large values, large throughputs... If a FoodWorld does not accept Gloderm, we are cut off from 20 outlets or 20,000 households. The supermarket is the trend of the future. A supermarket owner does not want to deal with different sales teams for each product group. He'll say send me one manager with whom I can place my orders for all your products for all my outlets. Are we geared for that?" asked Misra.

And that was what a supermarketer told him. "I am a big businessman with 20 stores that sell Rs. 25 lakh per month of all your products — from cosmetics to mosquito repellents and beverages. Are you going to offer me the same service that you were giving me when I was a one-store business and sold goods worth Rs. 4 lakh per annum?"

"So how can I help?" Misra had asked.

"I want one man from your company to deal with me. I don't want to deal with 30 different price lists. I may want different discount systems, different merchandise, different incentives... I may want a totally different reward scheme instead of the standard 5% retail margin. Don't forget I sell Rs. 25 lakh worth of your products."

So when push came to shove, some large retailers, particularly the supermarkets, had begun to launch their own brands. So Kuello was now competing with retailers' brands at the supermarkets. For example, a commodity like *atta* was being packaged and branded by the store. As a friend in a foodstuff firm told him: "My competitors in *atta* are no more regional like those in Gujarat or Maharashtra, but like this store brand."

Misra had seen this trend growing. "What more endorsement do you need?" Misra asked Gupta. "How are we geared, to this nascent but growing trend?"

Kuello, he felt, needed to look at distribution strategies and differentiated strategies for different types of markets. Trade in Chennai and Bangalore was highly developed; the number of supermarkets was growing there. In Mumbai, however, the concept was slow to take off, since space was at a premium there. But website or e-mail vending showed promise in the metropolis. For instance, retailers operating out of 300 sq.ft. shops could soon move to virtual shopping on the computer screen. "Mumbai may be the first city where large retail outlets could go out of style," said Misra. 'You will not need large space any more. Of course, the original theories on stocking and brand preferences will hold good. But the retailer is getting savvy. So you will need to get savvy too."

> Another important reason for shifting the focus to the retailer was the growth of supermarket chains, which could influence many more consumers.

And that meant changing the sales management structure, changing the incentive system from brands or products to total purchases from a company. Or separate schemes for different markets, even different stores. Because the retailer today had his own schemes to drive sales in his store. "And these may be different from what you may have in mind," said Misra. "Nanz, for instance, may offer two one-litre bottles of Coke free with purchases of above Rs. 1,000 of its store brands of pulses. How do you cope with that?" asked Misra.

The overpowering issue was the critical nature of the trade. More than selling the product, the retailers were selling a shopping experience. So in the case of the virtual reality shop, the consumer sought that shopping experience on the screen. "We need to anticipate the retailing trends which are fast catching on here. How do we gear our distribution to match that retailing pattern?"

Today the distribution strategies of most firms were geared to the retailing pattern. It was time to plan for the changing retail scene, felt Misra. "Appoint account managers who will focus on a single large account like a supermarket," he suggested. "Or three or four big volume outlets. He will address all orders — be it for mosquito repellents, floor hygiene care products, soaps or cosmetics." The focus on the big-ticket retailers was gaining ground. There were many single-shop retailers delivering big volumes. Like on Napean Sea Road in Mumbai, where new retailers were unlikely to come in, given the cost of property; three or four big outlets had volumes of Rs. 1.25 crore.

"In short, we must recast the entire sales approach," said Misra. "Therefore," he continued, "why not have a 'sales manager — key accounts', who will handle three or four big retail accounts? If we can have a territory manager for Chennai city which accounts for Rs. 8 crore in cosmetic sales, wouldn't a FoodWorld, a Nilgiris and another equally large account together be worth the same attention? Think about it."

Naturally, even the supermarkets themselves would want a central point of purchase for all their outlets. As the head of one supermarket said: "There are some items where I do not want to carry stocks. For instance, I want fresh *atta* whenever I ask for it. I am in a metro, why should I go through a stockist? Your factory should be able to deliver fresh stocks on demand."

When Gupta contacted the website supermarket, the owner said: "I will place my orders with you for all your products every Monday morning on e-mail. How your internal sales management is structured is not my concern. I want a single point of contact and prompt servicing. Because my USP is virtual time. If you can cope with that, great, we can do business together."

Analysis I: Sunder Hemarajani

TREAD CAUTIOUSLY

Sunder Hemrajani is executive director (sales), South Asia Business Unit, PepsiCo India Holdings.

'Partners in Business', 'Partners in Progress', 'First Customer' are different terms used by several companies to define their relationship with stockists. Literally, the terms may be different but the sentiment they connote is the same. Stockists are, indeed, one of the important stakeholders of a company. 'Stakeholders' are those with an interest or stake in a company's success. Stakeholders include shareholders, employees, suppliers, retailers and consumers.

Progressive companies evolve a strategic design which enables them to create value for all the stakeholders. In a way, all stakeholders are dependent on one another to be successful. Shareholder value can be achieved only through success in the marketplace... only if the retailers and consumers select your products and services instead of those offered by competitors.

However, the idea that stockists do not have a choice is quite dated. Stockists take on a company's business out of choice. Many companies have learnt this lesson the hard way. A loss of one good stockist can lead to a loss of 100 retailers and 1000 valuable consumers. Rajan Misra needs to tread cautiously while expounding on the primacy of the retailer.

Misra is trying to make Gupta aware of the changes in the consumers' buying behaviour and the evolution of trade channels. In a country like India, which has a well-dispersed population, the consolidation of trade has been slow but quite steady, especially in the large metros. The major bottleneck has been the lack of infrastructure. Chaotic conditions on the roads make it difficult for consumers to drive long distances to make purchases. Low labour cost enables your neighbourhood *kirana* shop to send a boy on a cycle to deliver one cake of soap at your doorstep. On the other hand, the trade continues to get fragmented in the rural areas where retailers are moving closer to consumers as the road network evolves. The channel architecture of multi-product companies like Kuello would need to recognise these diverse trends.

> The idea that stockist do not have a choice of companies is quite dated. Stockist take on a company's business out of choice.

Spiralling real estate prices in the metros have adversely impacted the growth of the retail trade. There is a slowing down of the consolidation process. Efficient servicing has become critical for getting higher penetration in the outlet.

> Sales organisations are meant to service the distribution system. They have to build skills in the system to get the firm a competitive advantage.

Misra seems to have understood that the trade service strategy would need to be reviewed in the light of changes in the trade scenario. The key questions he needs to answer are: which consumers would Kuello service in the future; through which channels will the company reach its consumers; what skills and competencies would Kuello need to build; and what is needed to build a long-term competitive advantage in reaching its consumers?

Servicing an online supermarket or a chain like FoodWorld, Nilgiris or Nanz would require a different set of skills and capabilities that are currently not present in the stockist system. Channel architecture would have to be flexible to cater to the evolving trade segments. Ignoring emerging segments, however tiny, could result in poor service and incomplete product range, or, worse, allow competition easy entry into consumers' homes.

Sales organisations are meant to service the distribution system. They all meant to build skills and capabilities in that system which could give a company competitive advantage. Restructuring a sales organisation to service evolving segments is not uncommon. Haven't we heard of a separate sales structure in most organisations to service the Canteen Stores Department (CSD) — a very large account for many companies.

Integration of businesses for servicing consolidated trade like supermarkets and chain stores, apart from improving the negotiating position of the supplier, can lead to a responsive and cost-effective service infrastructure, the benefits of which can be shared. A long-term relationship can be profitable for both if the parties work together to reduce costs in the supply-chain. Needless to say, the benefits are shared by all — marketer, retailer and consumer.

It is quite apparent that Misra would need to reorient the strategic architecture in the light of changes in the environment. Market leadership can only be achieved through:

- Leadership in trade satisfaction by delivering superior customer service.
- Penetration of key accounts and emerging trade segments.
- A high-quality selling organisation consisting of people with the requisite skills and sales processes built around IT which facilitate sales analyses and efficient services to the trade.

Analysis II: S. Murti

MONITOR THE NEW-AGE RETAILER

Shiv Murti is vice president, Great Wholesale Club, RPG's GIANT Hypermarket. He handles the merchandising portfolio for GIANT. He has a wide experience in marketing and supply-chain management in retailing.

Rajan Misra is futuristic managers who recognise the fundamental changes taking place in retailing. The quantum shifts which he envisages in the future are:

- Redefining who the customer is for the manufacture.
- Changes in shopping habits, specially the shift from *kirana* stores to supermarkets, since they offer more value to the end-consumer in terms of choice and convenience.
- Redefining the market in terms of shelf-space, since this directly reflects sales and also helps increase it.

Why does Misra think that the organised retailer is as important as a customer? These retailers are well-versed in the art of brand building and, in a very broad sense, manage more brands at any given point of time than the brand management teams of most large fast moving consumer goods companies. It is only logical that this mega brand management team should be adequately motivated to focus on a particular brand.

However, with improving technology, new products and variants are easier to launch and be copied by competitors. Therefore, it is all the more difficult to build a brand, as trials and usage are now split across more segments. The informative role of advertising is becoming increasingly difficult in the face of clutter and spiralling media costs. Hence, new products can grow into strong brands only if they are well supported at the points of purchase through display and promotion.

It is in this context that the role of the organised retailer assumes critical significance. Traditional 'mom and pop' stores in their 300-500 sq. ft. of space have obvious limitations with regard to display and point-of-purchase cues. They are slowly shifting from meeting the shoppers' monthly requirements to convenience. They are focusing on catering to the locality's convenience by keeping longer hours, offering smaller pack sizes, and so on.

In this situation, customers will increasingly turn to the large retailers/ *kirana* stores for their monthly requirements. However, these standalone stores might face increasing operational problems in terms of credit, manpower and so on. As in all other developing economies, customers will seek the 'touch, feel and see' experience in their quest for a better lifestyle and standard of living. And this experience can be provided only by modern supermarket chains.

Given these factors, Misra must seek a paradigm shift in the mindset of the sales team — from booking orders to servicing retailers. This partnership can flourish only if the sales teams understand what is important from the retailers' point of view and structure themselves to cater to these needs. It should focus on:

Supplies and Stocking Levels: Given the antiquated distribution systems in the country, erratic supplies are the norm. This regularly leads to stockouts, old stocks, and so on. This shortcoming stands exposed in a supermarket environment where every product has its own space, and if no stocks are available it is immediately noticed.

Misra must seek a paradigm shift in the mindset of the sales team — from booking orders to servicing retailers.

Organised retailing, by definition, gives more value to the end-customer by shortening the supply-chain and making it more efficient. This is done by having a centralised distribution system, where the supplies are received at a common single point and then redistributed to various stores, depending on demand. Thus, an organised supermarket also acts as a stockist for the company. This distribution structure requires a different kind of supply pattern, one which leverages the benefits of this centralised distribution rather than duplicating it.

Uniform Supply and Credit Terms: Supermarket chains have stores in different cities that co-ordinate with different sales managers of the manufacturer. At present, there is a wide variation in supply terms like credit periods, promotion, and so on. A partnership would eliminate these variations and lead to a more efficient and long lasting relationship.

New Products: New product packaging in our country is rarely designed keeping in mind the retailer's operational convenience. Varying heights of a category of products, for instance, lead to severe operational problems in terms of readjusting shelf-heights. Advance information on new products would enable the company to place them on the shelves of the stores faster.

To make this partnership meaningful there should be a parallel sales organisation reporting to a common sales and marketing head. This organisation should function like the client servicing team of an ad agency. The role of this team should be to drive sales by being the representatives of their respective supermarket chains in the manufacturer's organisation. It should also focus on value addition like training programmes for the store staff, special launch programmes, customer profiling for the supermarket chain and so on.

A national head of special accounts should be supported by a 'special accounts manager', based at places where the supermarket chains are headquartered, responsible for that particular chain of stores and supported by a sales team in each of the cities where the stores are located. This team should be supported by two functions:

Category Managers: They should plan for a particular category, to achieve category dominance by adopting a suitable basket of brands for the relevant supermarket chain based on the customer profile.

Marketing Analyst and Promotions Co-ordinator: He will analyse sales data, customer profile data, comparisons with the sales trends of the other retailers, and so on. He would be responsible for devising promotions specially tailored to meet the unique needs of that chain of stores. This person's job would involve extensive interaction with the sales team, the category managers as also the traditional functional teams.

Notes

Notes